Clean 500 PP!

Mottle W.
Coat on
cover

Our Sons, Our Heroes

Memories Shared by America's Gold Star Mothers from the Vietnam War

by
Linda Jenkin Costanzo

Given the subject matter, it continues to stir a wealth of emotions within me. The stories are sensitively written and the author sincerely cares about these mothers and their sons who died a half a world away. People need to know that the cost of war continues long after it officially ends. The pain and life-long struggles of these precious ladies and their families need to be told. I would wholeheartedly recommend this book for every American, especially those who served or had to deal with losing a loved one in a war. As a Vietnam Veteran, I am grateful that the author wrote this book.

Paul Fazekas, author of *Enduring Images: From the Trauma of War to Lifelong Healing*

Awesome…I'm lost for words.

Robert E. Wilczak, author of *Eye of the Eagle: Benedict Arnold*

This story brought back a lot of memories that seem to magnify how sad the times were. As I was reading, I kept thinking to myself— how would a person who did not live in these days react? Would it be similar to what the dark ages are to me? This is a great book.

Ted Wilkinson, Western Director, New York State Council, Vietnam Veterans of America

My wounded in action Vietnam veteran husband, Dexter Lehtinen, and I are so appreciative of Linda's efforts to document the stateside stories of our gold star mothers of the Vietnam War. You, the reader, will learn the definition of patriotism.

Ileana Ros-Lehtinen, Congresswoman, Chairman Emeritus, Foreign Affairs Committee, 27th District, Florida

These interviews and stories shed light on consequences of the Vietnam War that most Americans have never considered. Sharing these experiences and losses is indeed overdue. It is important for Vietnam veterans to finally get the respect they deserve. As a mother of two, these moving stories from the point of view of military mothers who experienced the greatest loss of all—the loss of a child—truly touch my heart. These women are incredibly strong and I want to thank the author for giving these gold star mothers a voice and providing the opportunity for their stories to be told.

Kathleen C. Hochul, Former Congresswoman, House Armed Services Committee, 26th District, New York

Hidden deep in their hearts was a portrait each gold star mother held of her son. Linda Jenkin Costanzo framed each portrait for the mothers to lovingly display.

Father Paul Steller, Diocese of Buffalo, New York

Designed by Rachel Gottorff

Cover and back photos by Susan M. Phillips
suephil14120@aol.com

Author portrait by Gordon James Image Makers

Cataloguing in Publication Data

Costanzo, Linda Jenkin.

Our sons, our heroes : memories shared by America's Gold Star Mothers from the Vietnam War / Linda Jenkin Costanzo. -- Clarence Center, NY : Sonrisa Press, 2013.

   p. ; cm.

   ISBN: 978-0-9891506-06

1. American Gold Star Mothers, Inc. 2. United States--Armed forces--Biography. 3. Mothers of war casualties--United States--Biography. 4. Vietnam War, 1961-1975--United States--History. 5. Vietnam War, 1961-1975--Casualties--History. I. Title.

UB403 .C67 2013   2013910372
363.34/983--dc23   1312

Sonrisa Press

Linda Jenkin Costanzo
P.O. Box 92
Clarence Center, New York 14032

www.sonrisapress.com
Facebook.com/OurSonsOurHeroes

This book was printed in the United States of America

Acknowledgements

I am grateful to the following people who encouraged me to pursue my interest in sharing the stories of gold star mothers from the Vietnam War:

All 16 mothers in this book who took their time to meet with me. By sharing first-hand accounts of their experiences, and letters from their sons, they have provided answers to the missing chapter of our country's involvement in Vietnam.

My late husband Dennis who never got to see my project completed. May he smile joyfully at its completion.

My sons, Brian and Joshua who patiently waited to see the outcome. They are now the age of the young men mentioned in this book. May they never forget the price these young men and their mothers paid for our government's decision to become involved in Vietnam, and may they see why Vietnam will always stir a pain within me.

The following friends who have been with me at every turn of the road and traversed every mountain and valley with me:

Sharon Merlette, an incredible friend who was always there for me and believed in me.

Cathy (Kate) Bloom who has known me since we were ten.

Nancy Wandowski who read my earliest version while raising two small children—an angel and a true spiritual friend.

Theresa Sergi who sat with me in ninth grade as the Vietnam War raged on, and who shared the same wish I did—to bring the young Americans home.

Melinda Schmidt, a true mentor and brilliant lady who selflessly spent two years critiquing my work—never giving up and always smiling.

Sue Phillips, an incredible photographer who quietly listened and patiently gave advice.

The Niagara Falls Writers Group of the Association of Professional Women Writers (APWW) who knew there was a story to be told.

Lois Vidaver who polished the final manuscript with her detailed editing.

Barbara S. Russo, Diane O'Brien, Susan Williams, and Susan Stoler who helped proofread until their eyes were crossed.

Chapter 77 Vietnam Veterans: Mike Walker who tirelessly arranged photos and formatted text over many cups of coffee and Paul Piotrowski who located various books and resources for me. They are both incredible Vietnam veterans who've never stopped serving our country. Bob Metz who introduced me to two gold star mothers. Chapter 77 AVVA President Linda Sopic for her support.

Bob Gianetti, an English professor who patiently edited my writing for two years and pointed the way to the APWW of Niagara Falls.

Lynn Dell for all the editing support in the early stages of this story.

Lt. Col. James Cochran (U.S.A.F. Ret.), a joy to work with, whose passion for military accuracy, kindness and respect will always be remembered.

Rachel Gottorff, graphic designer who diligently applied her creativity and artistic ability, making this book better than I imagined.

Edie Koch and Lynne Wallace-Lee of Basics2Bylines, my earliest writing friends who pointed to the internet for publishing possibilities.

Sallie Randolph for her legal advice and introducing me to a whole new vision of publishing.

Donna Stewart who remembers the loss of young men from our generation and who encouraged me to keep writing about it.

Jim Schueckler and Ken Davis who generously shared their photos from the VirtualWall.org, Ltd.

Mary Sorrels, an extraordinary English teacher who showed me the power of words.

Father Paul Steller, Diocese of Buffalo, New York who shared his time and spiritual wisdom during the years I worked on this project.

Millie Fancher who always encouraged me on my spiritual path.

My students at Leonardo da Vinci High School, Buffalo, New York and Erie Community College who kept asking me when my manuscript would be completed. I couldn't disappoint them.

Contents

Dedication

To the 16 gold star mothers on my journey who took the time to share their memories and to all gold star mothers who never had the opportunity to do so. May our country come to know the chapter of American history that has remained deeply hidden in their hearts.

"You listen deeply for only one purpose - to allow the other person to empty his or her heart. This is already an act of relieving suffering. To stop any suffering, no matter how small, is a great action of peace."

Thich Nhat Hanh, *Creating True Peace*
(New York: Free Press, 2003)

Prologue ~ How it all began

In March of 2000 my young sons and I were attending a children's play in Buffalo, New York at the Theatre of Youth. Seated next me was a soft-spoken, white-haired lady with beautifully coiffed hair who had accompanied her daughter and two grandchildren to the play. While waiting for the play to begin, she introduced herself as Lillian and we soon became engaged in a cheerful conversation. She proudly spoke of her four children and then the conversation took a turn. Her voice lowered as she softly mentioned that she had lost her younger son, Mark, in Vietnam at the age of 19.

For an instant I stared ahead, unable to move as her words sunk in. I couldn't imagine losing a teenage son in a war. She also struck a deep nerve, as if a hand from the past had gently tapped my shoulder and taken me back to a time filled with memories of the Vietnam War.

At that moment the theater grew dark and the play began. I wondered what Lillian would have told me if time had allowed. She appeared to be a lady of incredible faith. I also wondered if her sacrifice for our country had ever been recognized. As the play ended and we said goodbye, I wanted to learn more of her experiences. In the days that followed, she often crossed my mind. I couldn't recall her or her son's last name. I only remembered that his last name began with a "V." I never thought we would meet again.

Shortly afterwards I visited the Vietnam Memorial located at the Erie Basin Marina in Buffalo. I scanned the last names of 514 servicemen from Western New York who had sacrificed their lives in Southeast Asia. As I approached the "V"s, one name caught my eye—Mark Vanderheid. That was it. I went home and checked the phone book, hoping to contact Mark's mother. There was no listing of that last name.

In April of 2000, our local newspaper commemorated the 25th anniversary of the end of the Vietnam War. As I read the series of articles, I felt that hand from the past gently tapping my shoulder once again. It took me back to 1967 when I was an impressionable 15-year-old. I remember watching nightly news clips of young men in combat. It astounded me to think that many of them were teenagers—only three or four years older than I was.

Memories surfaced of news articles about young men from our area who had sacrificed their lives. Many had just graduated from high school a year or two earlier. Yet what I did not give serious thought to at the time was the grieving mothers of these young casualties. My heart filled with compassion for them.

These women, whose children had served proudly and acted on the strength of their convictions, stood at a pivotal point in our country's history. Public support was eroding as U.S. involvement in Southeast Asia became more controversial. A storm of criticism surged when television and local newspapers showed military honor guards escorting flag-draped caskets off planes to their final resting place.

Questions raced through my mind regarding the 58,220 mothers of these fallen heroes. I wanted to know what had happened to these women after they lost their sons in America's unpopular war. I wondered what they would tell me about themselves and their sons. What would they say to their sons now if they could? Perhaps the most important question—how did they find the strength to continue on?

A chapter of American history had been left out about our involvement in Southeast Asia—the personal price paid by mothers who had lost so much as a result of our involvement there. I later learned that mothers who lose sons or daughters while in service to our country are referred to as gold star mothers. Despite all the reading I had done, along with inquiries I had made of librarians and Vietnam veterans, I was still unable to find any stories told by gold star mothers from the Vietnam War. I discovered that nothing was written about their struggles because *no one had asked.* It was time to give them a voice.

In my quest for answers, I learned about an organization located in Washington, D.C. called the American Gold Star Mothers, Inc. (AGSM). Most people are unaware of AGSM—it isn't a club that any mother aspires to join. It is a non-denominational, non-profit and non-political organization founded in 1928 by a group of mothers who had lost sons in World War I. It is a service organization whose goals include perpetuation of the memory of their sons and daughters, assistance to veterans of all wars or conflicts, and promotion of peace and good will for the United States and all other nations. AGSM extends assistance to all gold star mothers when possible. Members attend veterans' events, volunteer at Veterans Hospitals, and fundraise for homeless veterans or those in need. If a gold star mother becomes a member of the organization, she is referred to as an American Gold Star Mother. Some gold star mothers chose not to become members for various reasons. Others were unaware the organization existed at the time of their sons' deaths. The following stories are told by members as well as non-members. All these mothers have served as models of strength and faith.

National headquarters gave me the name of an American Gold Star Mother in my area. After contacting her and listening to her story, I was introduced to others. My search led to mothers throughout the United States who willingly shared their stories.

All the mothers I interviewed expressed a deep faith in something larger that helped them endure one of life's most difficult trials. With the support of family, friends and community, they found the strength to move past their losses. Those who joined AGSM found much needed support, for who can know the pain a mother feels at having lost a child but another mother suffering from the same loss?

For 12 years I went about locating mothers who were willing to share their experiences. Memories, long-guarded in their hearts, came forth. I had finally uncovered our country's missing chapter, unaccounted for, never discussed, and deeply buried in the hearts of ordinary women with incredible strength and character. As I was drawing to the conclusion of this book, something remarkable happened. I reconnected with Lillian, the lady I met in the theater at the start of this journey. Her story is told later in this book.

The following stories are based on interviews I had with each of the mothers at their homes. They are not transcripts of the interviews, but retellings of their stories as I heard them, respecting all the facts and details I was given. Those whom I interviewed saw my account of our meeting before publication and gave me permission to tell their stories.

Linda Jenkin Costanzo

Corporal
Curtis Eugene Crawford, U.S.M.C.

Dunkirk, New York

G Company, 2nd Battalion, 3rd Marine Division

Quang Tri, Vietnam

KIA: February 28, 1967

Age: 19

"I could go home and cry my eyes out and become
an old woman who no one wants around—or I could
direct this energy in a meaningful manner."

- Shirley Popoff

I was nervous when I called American Gold Star Mother Shirley Popoff, mother of Corporal Curtis Crawford. Shirley was past president of Buffalo Chapter 26 of the American Gold Star Mothers organization. She became the first of many mothers who would tell me their stories. Shirley lived about 40 miles from me and was willing to share her story. She invited me to come visit on the following Friday. And so began my journey.

On a crisp October evening in 2000, I drove out to ski country in the southern tier of Western New York, and arrived at a small well-kept house nestled in the Boston Hills. I felt nervous as I walked up the sidewalk to the front door and rang the doorbell. A tall, silver-haired woman studied me through the storm door before unlocking and opening it. She was not smiling and I began to question what I was doing there. Shirley Popoff was formal and proper. Her stoic manner made me wonder if she had served in the military.

Shirley lived alone and the house was deafeningly quiet as I entered the living room. Faded photographs of a U.S. Navy sailor and a Marine adorned the fireplace mantel. She introduced them as her sons, Michael and Curtis Crawford. Six or seven medals surrounding a Purple Heart were displayed in a case on the wall. Along with them was a Gold Star lapel button, acknowledging the loss of her younger son, Curt, in Vietnam.

A scrapbook lay on the coffee table. Shirley picked it up and handed it over to me. I took it and stared at the cover for some time, feeling as if I were about to trespass on someone's heart. Her quiet voice drew my attention. She reassured me, "Go ahead. It's okay to open it." As I opened the cover and carefully turned each page, Curt's life unfolded before me.

At the beginning of the scrapbook was a piece of artwork—a house Shirley's son had drawn in crayon. He drew the house with a chimney. A section of paper where the smoke would have been was charred. Shirley smiled, recalling the day he showed the drawing to his father, who had been sitting in a chair with a lit cigarette. His dad's cigarette accidentally ouched the paper from behind. The drawing began to smolder exactly where the smoke rose in Curt's artwork. She laughed, recalling Curt's surprise and how he said, "Look! The chimney caught fire!" She then began her story.

****

Neither of my sons was drafted. They enlisted—in service to their country. My oldest son was Michael but we called him Mickey. He joined the Navy in 1964. My younger son, Curtis Eugene Crawford, enlisted in the U.S. Marine Corps a year later.

The brothers were close. Growing up, they were never more than five minutes away from one another. One always knew where the other was. Curt was a good kid. He was quiet, easygoing and did anything I requested. If I asked him to take out the garbage, I didn't have to ask him twice. I was proud of Curt's athletic abilities. He enjoyed a challenge and was in constant motion. He was very agile, as if he danced when he moved.

Curt's main interest was baseball and we would go to the baseball stadium to watch the semi-pro games. He especially enjoyed watching his hero, Bobby Wine, a rookie shortstop for the Buffalo Bisons. My son expressed an interest to pursue college baseball training. Ultimately, he decided to leave high school and enroll in the Marine Corps.

Though he was good in school, I think he was bored with academics and felt an obligation to serve his country. We were all deeply patriotic. Curt's dad, my former husband, was a Pearl Harbor survivor. We divorced when the boys were young, but we shared joint custody. Without my knowledge, Curt asked his father to sign a paper giving consent for him to join the Marines at age 17. I never thought that he'd drop out of school, but he did.

My son trained at Camp Lejeune and later went to Vietnam. He was very busy and wrote infrequently. Weeks would go by before I heard from him. A letter from him was always a surprise since they came so few and far between. I later realized this was a blessing in disguise, because a lapse in his writing would have upset me to no end. I tried to keep up on events in Vietnam when I didn't hear from him.

I watched the nightly news to see the latest developments in the war. One evening I was crocheting and my boyfriend Michael was having a cup of coffee when the evening news ended. Even though he loved Curt very much, he turned to me and said, "Shirley, you can't look at everything you see on the news and think about Curt. Every time anything comes up about Vietnam, you come to attention. I think it's time you turned the television off and went to bed." We said goodnight and Michael left.

The room became very quiet after that. I was sitting in a chair past midnight, when there was a sudden presence of someone standing behind me. It wasn't frightening at all or anything like that. It was as if someone was going to caress me. The feeling was one of incredible peace, of someone gently putting his or her arms around me—and holding me. My little feline friend Mr. Jiggs was on the floor nearby. Whenever the cat saw anything unusual, his tail would stand out like a pointer dog. Suddenly, Mr. Jiggs stood, staring right over my shoulder with his tail pointed up. I sat very still for some time. "Jiggsy, did you see it too? I think we'd better go to bed." The cat and I went to bed but we were up and down all night—until about 5:30 in the morning.

The following afternoon around 4:30, there was a knock on my door. It was my sister asking if I was all right. I assured her I was fine, but sensed urgency in her question. When I asked her who she had with her, she did not reply.

At that time, I lived in an apartment on the second floor of a double home in Buffalo. Leading up to my apartment was a stairwell that made a sharp turn on the second landing. I could feel that someone was coming up the stairs behind my sister. "Do you have Marines with you?" I asked her. Two men in uniforms stepped up to the landing. "You're here to tell me that Curt's dead, aren't you?"

They looked at me in surprise. "Did somebody call you?"

"No, nobody called me. I can't explain it. If I told you, you'd probably think I'm crazy."

The Marines gave few details about my son. I later pieced together what happened and concluded from one particular article that Curt was attempting to help an injured Marine. In my scrapbook is a news article containing the photo of another young serviceman. The obituary identifies him as a Marine from Cheektowaga, New York.

This young man lived about an hour from where we lived. Curt used to tell me of a comrade he was serving with in Vietnam who was particularly fond of sports. My son had asked me to cut out sports articles for his friend. He and my son were killed on the same day, February 28, 1967. I later received his Silver Star medal and this citation:

> The enemy was well dug-in and was able to put out
> such a volume of small arms and automatic weapons
> fire that the company was pinned down. Under a hail
> of hostile fire, Corporal Crawford, a machine gun

squad leader, brought his guns forward and set them up on the left flank of his platoon's most forward positions, only 40 meters from enemy emplacements. From this position, he caught sight of a Marine who had been wounded during one of the earlier assaults. Unhesitatingly, he bounded forward, exposing himself to enemy fire to render assistance to the fallen Marine. As he cleared his cover an enemy sniper opened up from close range, wounding him in the leg and knocking him to the ground. Ignoring his wound, Corporal Crawford was able to whirl and send a lethal burst of rifle fire into the sniper's spider hole, killing him. He then continued to move forward to the Marine casualty. He had advanced only several more meters when he was fired upon again and mortally wounded.

I suspect the Marine who Curt was trying to save that day was his friend from Cheektowaga.

A week later, a U.S. Marine Corps body guard escorted Curt's body from Dover Air Force Base in Delaware to Buffalo. I followed the motorcade from Buffalo to Dunkirk. The Marine Corps major in charge of the procession said that it wasn't necessary for me to be there, but I felt it was. The hour drive was a long one. The shock of losing a son to war is something that no mother is prepared for. Thirteen days after he was killed, my son was buried on my birthday, March 13. He rests in St. Hedwig's Cemetery, in Fredonia, New York.

I think 1967 was the worst year of my life. After losing Curt in Vietnam in February, I worried about my oldest son, Mickey, stationed with the Navy in Norfolk, Virginia. He came home on emergency leave for Curt's funeral. When he left, I had no idea where he would be stationed. Shortly after, Mickey told me he volunteered to go to Vietnam. I was stunned. I had just lost Curt on February 28th, and now Mickey gave me this news. He shipped out on the USS Forrestal, first heading for the Mediterranean Sea and then on to the Gulf of Tonkin, off the coast of Vietnam.

Five months later, the morning of July 29, I was getting ready for work when there was a radio news bulletin. "We interrupt this program to say that the third largest aircraft carrier, the Forrestal, is a holocaust of flames…"

I sat there in shock. I stared off for some time, thinking—Oh my God, not again. When I came to my senses, I looked at the table and realized that I'd poured two separate cups of coffee. I reminded myself—Hey! There's only one person living here!

I remember wandering around the house putting my work clothes on over my nightgown. I collected my thoughts and called ship information. It was a futile attempt, but it was the only thing I could think of at the moment that might ease my mind. I told them I had a son on that ship and I asked how bad the fire was but it was too early to say. They couldn't give me any information. They only said that the situation was bad. It turned out that 134 men died.

I contacted the Naval Department and gave them my work number. I told them where I was going to be, in case they needed to contact me. I had to work that weekend, so I proceeded to go in, but I waited desperately to hear from someone. It was agony. From the morning that I heard the news on the radio, I began a new routine. Whenever I had a short break at work I'd call the Naval Department to see if there was any word about Mickey.

During this time, I was training a new operator for the phone company where I worked in Buffalo. She must have thought I was strange because everyday for a week I left promptly at noon when my lunch hour began. I'd hurry off to mass at Saint Paul's Cathedral, so I could be alone. It was a dark, uncertain time. As a person of faith, you don't get through the difficult times like this unless you believe that God is with you.

After a week of waiting, I entered my apartment one evening and the phone rang. I walked over and picked up the receiver. I heard the operator say, "I have a collect call for you from Subic Bay."

When I realized it wasn't the Naval Department, I breathed a sigh of relief and accepted the call. Mickey was calling to say he was in the Philippine Islands while the Forrestal was in port for repairs. He was staying there with his friend Chris, a shipmate. Chris's mother was going to prepare a "Christmas in July" celebration. Later, he would return to the States for a leave. It truly seemed like Christmas for me—my son was alive.

At work, the day after I received Mickey's call, I was so joyful that he was alive, I had to share the news with someone. It was Friday and I called the newspaper. I spoke with the City Editor, hoping something would be written about my son's survival on the Forrestal. "We don't consider the Forrestal as news anymore," the editor told me.

I asked that man for his name. When he told me, I thanked him and hung up. I went upstairs to tell the girl I had been training that she was ready to work the switchboard by herself. I explained I was going out on my lunch hour to take care of some business. I started out for the City Editor's desk, so incensed that I thought I was going to be arrested.

I was livid. I stormed into the lobby of the newspaper office and hurried over to the receptionist's desk. Acting flustered, I fibbed and told the receptionist I had an appointment with the news editor and I was running late. I asked for the quickest way to his office. She showed me to the elevator and ushered me in. I got off the elevator and proceeded into his office.

I introduced myself as the mother of a Forrestal survivor and I continued, "So, this is what a 24-carat jerk looks like! In other words, since we still have young men on the Forrestal who survived a terrible fire, you don't consider that news anymore? But you can publish fillers about how many potatoes are eaten in Czechoslovakia and things like that? Well, I have news for you! My son survived the fire on that ship and he's alive! There had better be something in the paper about it—a full-page ad."

"Lady, do you know how much an ad costs...," he said.

But I cut him off. "Don't even bother to ask! Do you know how much it costs to lose a son? My youngest son has already been killed in Vietnam, and I've gone almost a week thinking my other son had been killed too. And you have the gall to tell me that those who survived the ship fire aren't news! Well I've got news for you! There are people who think it is news! I expect to see something published about my son, a survivor of the Forrestal." I stormed out. I don't know if an article was published, but at least I felt the satisfaction of giving that editor a piece of my mind.

Many people still harbored an anti-war sentiment, and they were quick to come forward with their opinions. I never imagined that I would encounter harassment over such a personal loss. During lunch hour, I encountered local college students protesting on the streets in downtown Buffalo. They belonged to an anti-war group called Students for a Democratic Society. They would read the obituaries and search for names of servicemen like Curt and then place calls day or night to the families, venting anti-war sentiments. I received many of those calls.

One day, I called the Marine Corps office downtown and explained the situation of harassment from the students. I told the officer that I was going to go down to the university the following day to take this matter up with officials at the administrative office. He or any other Marines were welcome to come with me if they cared to. He said they would be happy to accompany me.

That evening, before I had the opportunity to settle the matter, the phone rang. Michael Popoff was visiting and answered it. It was another harassment call from a protester, venting his sentiments about the Vietnam War. Sensing that Michael was upset, I took the phone from him and blurted out, "I know the group that you're with. I don't know exactly where you're calling from, but I do know where you go to school, and I'm coming up there tomorrow with the Marine Corps officers. I'm going to have the joy of beating the hell out of you. If you or any of your cohorts ever call this number again, you will find out what hell is because I am it!" That was the end of the calls at home, but I was extremely sensitive to the anti-war sentiment in public.

One summer evening, I got home from work and put my dress shoes on to meet Michael at our favorite little diner on South Park Avenue. Two men were there when we arrived. One man, seated at the counter near the entrance, had fairly long blond hair but was neat in appearance. Seated on a stool, at the other end of the counter, was a man dressed in a three-piece business suit. Michael and I took our seats. "There's a Marine laid out at Nightengale's Funeral Parlor down the street," he said.

"He must have been killed in Vietnam," I answered.

Upon hearing my reply, the man in the business suit turned to us and commented loudly from the other end of the counter. "He got what he deserved."

I stood up and walked over to him. "What did you say?" He quickly got up and darted for the door. I chased him down South Park Avenue! He got away from me so I turned and went back to the café. There's no telling what I would've done had I caught up to him.

Looking back on it, I'd laugh too if I saw a middle-aged woman in high heels chasing a well-dressed young man down the street. When I re-entered the diner, the blond guy was laughing so hard he could barely control himself. Still enraged over the businessman's comment, I turned to the blond guy. "And you, Goldilocks, what do you find so funny?"

The young man's polite response gave him away. "Not a thing, ma'am!"

I knew instantly that this young man was a former serviceman. He had let his hair grow out after his military discharge so he would fit in at home. If he went out in public with a military haircut, he'd be identified as a Vietnam veteran. He would've been ostracized and at the mercy of public criticism. This was the type of harassment Vietnam veterans lived with when they returned home.

The painful process of dealing with my loss had only just begun. In quiet moments, with no one around, I reflected on my son, Curt. After his death, I often went outside late at night behind my apartment and sat on top of the garbage cans. I used to stare up at Heaven and look at each individual star. I felt that I was able to talk with Curt. There was some communication. I felt that somehow he knew I could talk to him. I felt closer to him and that, somehow, he could hear me.

To deal with my grief, I placed Curt's Marine Corps photo, votive candles, an American flag, and some of his medals for heroism on a table in the foyer of my apartment. One evening Michael came in. "I'm going to tell you one thing. You're probably going to blow your stack, but I'm telling you this for your own good and for your other son, Mickey. The first thing that everybody sees when coming through the door is that shrine you built to Curt. Break it up. Put it where you want, but don't make a shrine out of it. What do people think as they come through that door? What do you suppose Mickey thinks?"

It never occurred to me that perhaps Mickey thought I had more feelings for Curt than for him. I suddenly realized how deeply parents' overwhelming grief impacts the siblings of war casualties. The parents are focused on dealing with their own loss. The siblings don't just lose their brother. They feel slighted—as if they've lost their parents' love and attention as well. I followed Michael's suggestion. I put Curt's portrait in my bedroom and I placed the other items throughout my house.

In 1968, about a year after Curt's death, my boss called me in at work one day and told me there was a doctor there to give me a check-up. This surprised me. I wasn't due for my yearly exam, but I went in to talk with him anyway. If I remember correctly, this doctor had served in the Navy and he had experience dealing with trauma. He asked me questions like whom I lived with and talked to at home. I told him I lived alone and I talked to Mr. Jiggs, my cat.

He replied, "No, I mean human. Whom do you talk to?" I told him I live my evenings quietly with no one around.

What he said next hit me hard. "You are in denial of your son's death." I was startled at such a statement and told him it wasn't true. Ever so quietly he said, "Curt is dead. He's not here. He's never coming back. You'll never hold him again. He's not going to knock on your door."

I just sat there, numb. I was in there for two hours and did I ever cry. I had always felt it necessary to keep my composure for Mickey's sake. I thought I was coping well by keeping my thoughts of Curt to myself. But I don't think I really acknowledged my grief until that moment.

He persisted, asking if I had a hobby, and I said I enjoyed painting.

"Painting what?" he asked.

"I'm doing a painting of Curt," I replied.

"I want you to go home and put that portrait away. You paint anybody or anything that you want to, but you do not paint Curt. Do not bring it out. Pack it away and start painting something else, anything. But do not look at the painting of him anymore."

I continued to cry in front of him for the longest time. He probably handled the situation in a fair manner, but it didn't seem fair at the time. He touched on something that I had never spoken about with anybody.

But after that day with the doctor I started to come to terms with my loss. I went home, put my painting away and never took it out again. I never realized before how much I hurt inside. I spoke to the doctor occasionally after that. He said a boiling cauldron was buried deep within me and I kept it well hidden, but if I didn't do something about it, it would tear me apart. He suggested I become involved in the American Gold Star Mothers organization. That was excellent advice because I recall clearly when I looked at Curt's body for the last time, I told myself I could go home and cry my eyes out, and become an old woman who no one wants around—or I could direct my energy in a meaningful manner.

The AGSM organization isn't well known. It receives very little publicity, which is understandable. My first recollection of American Gold Star Mothers was when I was a little girl, watching a parade during the 1930s. Seeing ladies dressed in white uniforms and caps, riding in parade cars, I asked my mother who they were, and why silence came over the crowd when the women passed by. She whispered, "I'll explain to you later." My mother later told me they were mothers who had lost sons in the

Great American War, now known as World War I. The silence was an act of reverence when the mothers appeared at events.

My son was one of 514 Western New York casualties from the Vietnam War. However, there weren't even 200 mothers actively involved in local chapters. I had to inquire at an American Legion Post before I was directed to the Buffalo Chapter. I joined and began doing volunteer work at the Veterans Administration (VA) Hospital. That was rewarding for me because I've always had a special place in my heart for those who served in Vietnam. They came home so traumatized and psychologically wounded, I felt it was an honor to help them in any way I could. They've accepted me like a second mother. My goal has been to be of service to those who have served our country.

The veterans have become like sons to me. One of the guys at the VA nicknamed me "Tough Mother," after seeing a billboard advertisement of a gray-haired granny wearing name-brand blue jeans. I had the demeanor of a rugged, independent woman—someone who could hold her own when necessary. As time went on, the name stuck. The guys at the hospital still call me that.

I remember when I learned that the water fountains on a floor of the VA Hospital needed repair. Water came up warm and then dribbled down the spout. The men were covering the fountain spouts with their mouth in order to drink. I blew my stack and inquired about the problem at the desk. They told me, "Oh, yes. We put in work orders to have the fountains fixed, but nothing's been done."

I insisted that the administration get bottled water immediately, before an epidemic broke out. These men were taking medication and to think that they didn't have access to fresh, cold water outraged me. It was immediately taken care of. I never would have known the needs of these young men and women if I hadn't volunteered there.

A few years later, a doctor at the VA Hospital asked me if I'd like to work in the Post Traumatic Stress Disorder (PTSD) Unit with a group of eight or ten guys who had returned from Vietnam. I told him I wasn't qualified. I lacked a degree and counseling experience. He said I would be most qualified, having been through all that I had. I accepted the challenge and it was among the most rewarding experiences of my life. It gave me great satisfaction to see progress when I worked with those young men from 1968 through 2000. It was the least I could do for them. They were just 18 and 19 year old kids when they went to Vietnam, and they wound up going through so much.

I served as president of Buffalo Chapter 26 and later served as department president for New York State. During that time, I attended national conventions where I met hundreds of other American Gold Star Mothers. They shared similar experiences to mine, and we gave each other support.

In 1976, nine years after Curt's death, I married Michael Popoff. He was most understanding of my loss. Michael and I made our first trip to The Wall in Washington D.C., the day after it was dedicated on Veteran's Day, November 11, 1982. The nine-hour drive felt like we were going to a major funeral. We didn't speak the entire trip and I didn't know what awaited us. It was a quiet, overcast day with few people in attendance. The grass had been flattened from the crowd attending the opening ceremony the day before.

After viewing The Wall, Michael and I traveled to Colonial Williamsburg in Virginia. I noticed a group of young adults with Down Syndrome also sightseeing. I was standing outside a stable when I spotted a young man, about 19, looking in awe at the horses inside. I asked him if he had seen the big horses. "Oh-h yeah!' was all he could say in his hushed tone of excitement. I was drawn to the delight on his face as he saw such a large animal up close. I asked him if he had ever touched the nose of such a giant. He quickly replied, "Oh-h no." I explained that the horse wouldn't bite. I gently encouraged him to venture forward and touch the animal's velvet-soft nose, which he did. He seemed at a loss for words. "Oh, nice!" was all he could say.

He walked back to his group, said something to his group leader, then came back—and put his arms around me. The group leader looked shocked, but I assured her it was okay with me. I told her we had been on a solemn journey to The Wall, and it had been so quiet because I had been unable express how I felt ever since I lost Curt. But that young man's hug made my day.

He was so special. I marveled that he could feel such innocence and joy at something as simple as petting a horse. It was the touch from his hug that broke the ice forever, the ice that surrounded my heart after losing Curt 15 years before. The rest of that November trip was Heaven.

It has been 33 years and despite the painful loss, I can still feel close to Curt. My life changed dramatically after I lost him, but by becoming involved and honoring his memory, many special events kept me connected to him.

****

Shirley's story of Curt had gone full circle. I still wanted to know what she would say to Curt now. She stared off for several moments as if in a trance. Silence descended in the room and I barely breathed. She carefully chose her words and then softly replied:

"I hope that I was the mother you deserved because I loved you very much. The ghosts in my bedroom came each night when I would go to bed worrying. They came for both you and Mickey. I wondered what situations you both faced. You did what you wanted. You fulfilled your duties honorably. Curt, you went out to save one of your fellow Marines. I couldn't have asked you to do more. In my opinion, you are my angel and my hero. Your brother Mickey is my angel and my hero, also. Someday we will be able to communicate. I love you both."

****

That evening cemented a friendship with Shirley Popoff. She became a close confidant as well as a "grandmother" to our sons who also refer to her as "Tough Mother." Shirley took me under her wing. Sensing that others would share their memories also, she invited me to a meeting of the Buffalo Chapter of American Gold Star Mothers held at a VFW post in South Buffalo. I gratefully accepted and later attended the meeting of six mothers. Like most posts, aging World War II veterans sat at the bar. Each one nodded respectfully to the American Gold Star Mothers as they passed through on their way to the meeting.

The meeting started with a candle lit in honor of those they lost. Shirley introduced me and I was warmly welcomed. The agenda that followed included a statement of my purpose for being at the meeting. After the meeting, three ladies said they would be glad to share their stories. But before I had the opportunity to meet them, I received a call and instead, accepted an invitation to meet two American Gold Star Mothers from New Jersey.

And so my journey continued and resulted in the writing of this book.

Shirley Popoff

Sergeant
Joseph Frank Biber,
U.S.M.C.

E Company, 3rd Reconnaissance Battalion,
3rd Marines

Santa Clara, California

Quang Tri, Vietnam

KIA: September 19, 1968

Age: 22

"I just wish every gold star mother had been given the opportunity to join this worthwhile organization."

- Ann Biber

I'd like to thank American Gold Star Mother Judith Young of Moorestown, New Jersey, who introduced me to Ann Biber, Mary Korona, and Virginia Dabonka, three American Gold Star Mothers from her state.

Judith met me at the Philadelphia Airport on a bitter cold, bright December morning. We piled my luggage into her van and headed out for northern New Jersey. The ride in a warm, comfortable van afforded me the opportunity to see how the city and suburbs changed into rolling hills dotted by an occasional house. I never realized New Jersey was so large, hilly and beautiful.

After a three-hour drive, the van climbed a steep, country road and stopped in front of a one-story home. Judith explained that we were going to meet Ann Biber, mother of Sergeant Joseph Biber, U.S.M.C. Joseph's younger brother, Frank, owned the house. He and his family lived in the left half while Ann lived in the right.

A neatly dressed lady with glasses and conservatively-cut white hair greeted us at the door. Ann introduced herself with a businesslike manner. I could see why she had served as national president of the AGSM organization.

As we entered the kitchen, I scanned a wall covered with dozens of Christmas cards. I was impressed with the quantity of cards and the care with which they were displayed. Ann noticed my look of admiration. She smiled proudly and informed me that the Christmas cards were from gold star mothers she had befriended through the years. I sensed a sisterhood of support in her words.

Knowing our timetable and the distance we had yet to cover that day, we wasted no time getting started. I sat in the swivel rocker facing Ann in her cozy living room. I noticed a frame containing military medals displayed on a shelf behind her.

I had to listen closely as Ann answered my questions. She cautiously thought her answers through, but delivered her replies with a rapid-fire and charming New Jersey accent. Ann knew what she wanted to say. In a controlled tone, she shared her story with me.

****

I always affectionately referred to my son Joseph as the tall, skinny kid with the brown eyes. He was the second oldest of five children. His older sister enjoyed her position at the top of the sibling totem pole and made sure Joseph knew it. He always rose to the occasion when she challenged him and they argued often. Maybe it was his nature—he had his share of disagreements with his younger sister as well, and their differences didn't always end diplomatically.

Our lives were thrown into turmoil when Joseph's dad and I went through a divorce. When his dad left for California, Joseph wanted to go with him, but his dad disapproved. At the time, I didn't want my son to go either. Joseph was hurt and deeply resentful as he remained in New Jersey with my younger son, my daughters, and me.

Our lives settled down after his dad left. We heard little from him, and Joseph seemed fine. But the minute my son heard from his father he would get all worked up. He insisted on living with his dad. Finally, when he was 12, I told myself that before he gets into real trouble I might as well let him go. I was working by then. My mother was watching all four kids, and she couldn't handle Joseph. Reluctantly, I gave in to his wishes. I worried about my son's well-being since he'd be living so far away.

In spite of my concerns, Joseph did well there. He put his energy to good use by joining the track team at Buchser High School in Santa Clara, California. He thrived on competition and was Buchser High's fastest runner for the mile, with a time of 4:22. His time for the two-mile run was 9:32. He placed among some of the best runners in the nation. His time and effort on the track team paid off. He was recognized for his outstanding athletic ability and received a scholarship to Idaho State University when he graduated in 1964.

Joseph didn't say what he wanted to major in, but he took history, thinking it would be an easy subject. I guess he found out otherwise because he didn't do well in his classes. He attended college for six months and then dropped out in January 1965. That meant he lost his scholarship. Leaving college meant he also lost his military deferment.

He returned to New Jersey to live with my daughters, my younger son Frank, and me. It had been seven years since he left with his dad and I was happy to have him home again. He worked for six months before he received his notice from the draft board to report to the Army. He had to return to California where he originally registered. The Marines were looking for volunteers at the time, so my son got a release from his obligation to the Army and enlisted in the Marines. He began basic training in January 1966, and by spring of that year, he left for Vietnam. He finished his first tour of duty in March 1967. He returned home and immediately had knee surgery, leading me to believe that he was done with combat duty overseas.

Following his surgery, my son worked as a military prison guard for a year. He came home on leave in spring of 1968, but he said nothing about his plans as his furlough ended. I presumed he was returning to his job at the prison. As he started packing, he suddenly announced that he was going back to Vietnam for a second tour of duty. I was stunned. When I asked him why he wanted to go back, all he said was, "The prison job isn't for me. I want to go back to Vietnam. I can do more good over there than I can here in the United States."

He spent his second tour of duty with the 3rd Reconnaissance Battalion along the Demilitarized Zone (DMZ) that separated North and South Vietnam. His second tour was scheduled to end in December. He had three months left when he was killed.

The Marines notified Joseph's father in California first. His dad called my home but reached our younger son, Frank, with the news. Frank contacted me at the home of a family where I worked as a babysitter. The Marines also phoned me and offered to pick me up and take me home. I was grateful for their concern, but I had just moved to the town of Wayne, New Jersey and was unable to explain directions for them to locate me so I declined their offer. I explained that I'd be all right and would be able to get home by myself.

I mustered the strength to function during the chaotic moments that followed the tragic news. I knew very few people since I was new to the area. My daughters had homes of their own. Frank was the only one still living at home with me. Joseph's dad made the funeral arrangements, so our son was buried in Totowa Boro, New Jersey. Unfortunately, I had little say in the matter. I would've preferred to have my son buried in a military cemetery, such as Arlington, yet in some ways, it comforts me knowing he is buried in Totowa Boro, because my baby girl is buried there, also.

When the Marines notified me of Joseph's death, they had few details. I later learned that on September 19, 1968, my son was on a reconnaissance mission, leading a group of about eight Marines. He was second in line behind the point man. The point man's job is to scout up ahead, making sure it's clear before signaling back to the leader who, in this case, was Joseph. As he was waiting to move the eight men forward, there was an exchange of gunfire up ahead. The point man kept quiet and hid from view. Joseph and the men behind him stopped and waited for him to signal. After a long wait, Joseph didn't see or hear from him so he moved forward to find him. That was when the enemy opened fire.

I learned more when I read the book, *Never Without Heroes* [Lawrence C. Vetter, Jr., New York: Ivy Books, 1969]. Vetter had served with Joseph in the same unit. According to the author, when the enemy fired, my son was hit in the artery of his upper leg. They airlifted him out on a helicopter, but he lost a considerable amount of blood and died en route to the hospital. Joseph was posthumously awarded the nation's third highest medal, the Silver Star.

I have always felt that kids need to be raised with a sense of commitment and leadership. I am proud of my son for serving our country. He displayed leadership and courage to those he served with, and he sacrificed his life for them. I think his commitment to our country left a deep impression on those around him. My younger son, Frank, for example, has provided a home for me next door to him and his family. I had told my children that if they want anything I own, they should let me know and I'd make sure they'd get it after I was gone. Frank's only reply was, "I want all of my brother's stuff."

As a single mother, I look back on the years of raising my four kids and I feel that the government could be more supportive financially. During WW II there was something called a Mother's Pension. My mother received it after my brother Joseph died in WW II. It was a small monthly stipend available to gold star mothers if they had lost their sons in a war and had no one left to support them. In order to qualify, a gold star mother's income could not exceed $1,800 per year. Problems arose because the requirement to obtain the stipend hadn't been updated since World War II. By the time the Vietnam War was on, mothers' salaries often exceeded $1,800 and therefore they didn't qualify.

I would like to see all gold star mothers receive the stipend. The AGSM organization feels strongly about the issue and we've worked to change the legislation. A change was proposed before the year 2000, allowing all gold star mothers to receive this pension regardless of their income. It has been delayed by Congress, though, and has not passed yet. I'm grateful for the effort and support of my fellow American Gold Star Mothers, and hope that legislation concerning the Mother's Pension will be enacted by the government.

My affiliation with the AGSM organization began years before I lost my son Joseph in Vietnam. I learned about it when I was a young girl, growing up during World War II. My older brother Joseph, who was my son's namesake, was killed in Germany in 1945 and buried in Holland. My mother joined AGSM organization and helped start a chapter in Paterson, New Jersey.

I learned a lot from watching her and I met many World War II American Gold Star Mothers who joined the Paterson chapter. As the years passed, the mothers often lost their husbands or they became disabled, so I used to help out by driving them to appointments or assisting them as they grew older. I always felt close to them and I was still helping many of them when my son passed away. For that reason, I immediately joined the organization.

I received a warm welcome from these ladies. Our chapter is a tight-knit group and includes several Vietnam era mothers. I've been active in the organization for 32 years. I've served as president on the state level, I've served on the board of directors for five years, and eventually, I served as National President in 1990.

When I joined the AGSM organization in 1968, the membership was roughly 23,000 mothers. At that time, most of them had lost sons in World Wars I and II but there were some mothers from the Korean and Vietnam Wars. Oddly, our membership never increased as the Vietnam War continued. We lost over 58,000 Americans in Vietnam, so we knew there were several thousand gold star mothers who were not getting the support of our organization.

As of the year 2000, the AGSM enrollment was about 1,000 members. I think there are two main reasons for this decline. First, many mothers were unaware the AGSM organization existed during the Vietnam War. When the Defense Department notified the families about their sons, it refused to include a brochure about our organization. We tried to get the government to hand out a brochure to the gold star mothers, explaining the purpose of our organization and extending the invitation to join. The government refused to do it as well, saying it's the Defense Department's responsibility. If we'd been able to contact the mothers, or if they had known about us, I'm sure we could've reached many more mothers at the time. They shouldn't have had to *seek out* the organization. The mothers should've been *given* this information.

There was a second reason for the declining membership. In some chapters, mothers who lost sons in the Vietnam War weren't openly welcomed. Some American Gold Star Mothers from World Wars I and II gave a cool reception to those who lost sons in the Vietnam War, stating in effect, it really wasn't a *declared war* at all, but a *conflict*. Consequently, new gold star mothers from the Vietnam War were occasionally snubbed by older mothers, making them feel they didn't warrant membership in the organization. This is the other reason our organization lacks so many members from the Vietnam War. Speaking for my chapter in New Jersey, we never had this problem. We got along well, regardless of the war our sons served in. However, the elitist attitude of a few did great harm to the organization's membership.

As a result, thousands of gold star mothers missed the opportunity to receive support and comfort from our organization. The membership dwindled and now it's too late. If the AGSM organization were to try to enlist the gold star mothers from the Vietnam War, their reply might be, "If you didn't want us years ago, why do you want us now?" The truth is, we would've loved to have all gold star mothers from the Vietnam War join us. It was a loss not only to our organization but for those who didn't join. Our organization provides incredible support.

I have met many wonderful people through the ASGM organization that I never would've known otherwise. The dozens of Christmas cards on my wall are indicative of the friends I've made. Each card symbolizes not only a son or daughter who died in service to their country, but a mother who sacrificed also.

I have always felt a deep loyalty to our country and will remain committed to reaching out to gold star mothers who've experienced the same loss that I've had. By volunteering in the AGSM organization, I received a great deal in return. It has been a tremendous support group, offering positive benefits. Giving back helped me in my darkest moments. I consider myself a person of faith and relied on my spiritual strength to survive the loss of Joseph. You have to have faith in order to go on from one day to the next.

****

When asked if there was anything else she cared to comment on about her experiences as an American Gold Star Mother, Ann paused for several moments. Looking out the window, she searched carefully for words. She replied in a soft, sad tone:

"There were an awful lot of young men killed in Southeast Asia. I just wish that every gold star mother had been given the opportunity to join this worthwhile organization."

****

Ann Biber was a beacon of encouragement for mothers who have traveled the same path that she did. She passed away suddenly in late 2002, two years after I met her. The Mother's Pension that she strongly advocated never reached Congress for a vote. The only state that now provides a pension for parents is Massachusetts. A check for $1,000 is sent out on April 1 and on August 1, to every gold star mother and gold star father. Such a law has not been passed in other states.

Ann Biber with Joseph's medals

Specialist 4
Albert Korona III,
U.S. Army

A Company, 39th Infantry, 9th Infantry Division

Trenton, New Jersey

KIA: May 18, 1967

Long An, Mekong Delta, Vietnam

Age: 20

"I volunteered at the VA hospital. I'd like to think if it were my son laying there, another mother would try to help him."

- Mary Korona

When Judith Young and I left Ann Biber's house, the afternoon sunshine illuminated the New Jersey hills. By the time we arrived in Trenton, darkness had fallen and an icy, relentless wind was bending the brittle branches of the trees.

We pulled in to a nearly empty parking lot and faced a fortress-like brick high-rise for senior citizens. I was struck by the bitter cold and the black sky, which contrasted with the glittering stars above me. I wanted to gaze at them, but my thoughts were on the lady inside who had waited for us all day.

Silence enveloped us inside the dimly-lit building. We took an elevator to the fifth floor, where we were hit by a blast of warm air. We knocked on the metal door and it took several minutes before a chain slipped off and the door opened.

Mary Korona, a frail, petite lady, barely five feet tall, greeted us with a smile and ushered us in. Showering us with kindness, she told me to pick any seat. I silently scanned the room, trying to see which would be best for her. She read my mind. "Oh, don't worry about me. I can sit anywhere."

Embarrassed by her keen observation, I quickly picked a chair. "How about a glass of water or something to drink?" she asked. Judith and I told her not to fuss, but her insistence wore us down and I opted for a glass of water. I held my breath as the frail octogenarian maneuvered across the living room with a glass of water in each hand.

She listened intently as I explained the purpose of my writing. Her eyes sparkled with curiosity as she asked, "So, you put the names of the soldiers in the story?" I smiled and assured her that her son's name would be in the story. She immediately began talking about her son and, for an hour, time disappeared as she spoke of "Bunny."

****

We named him Albert Korona III, but we always called him Bunny. One year, when he was a toddler, we put him into a hooded snowsuit and zipped him up. We stepped back to see how he looked and what a comical sight! His brown curls poked out from the hood and a big grin revealed two baby teeth. He looked just like the Easter Bunny. From that day on, he had a nickname. He later grew to be 6 feet 4 inches, yet it never bothered him to be called Bunny by his teenage friends.

My son was always on the go. He loved to devise ways to escape from

Larry, his younger brother of two years. Bunny teased him to tears and never wanted to take Larry along with him. He preferred to do everything with his friends, including horseback riding.

My son was a jokester and amused us with imitations of television characters such as Frankie Fontaine and Ed Sullivan. He imitated our family and his friends as well. It didn't matter who they were—he was good at it.

Summers were very special for us, especially when the boys were small. During the school year we lived in the city of Trenton, New Jersey, but we had a summer home in Brown's Mills near Fort Dix. The day after school let out, we'd leave the city and we didn't return until the day before classes began in September. From our Fort Dix home, we could see the soldiers across the fields out on the shooting ranges. Bunny and Larry had the chance to see the soldiers up close practicing their daily drills on the road in front of our house.

My sons decided that a secluded tree house in a big shade tree would be an ideal spot for a "fort." They took water pistols up the tree with them and waited for the right moment when the soldiers marched beneath them. From their hidden fortress, they squirted the soldiers. Fortunately these were hot summer days so no one ever objected.

One day as summer came to a close, Bunny seized the opportunity to talk to the soldiers. My husband used to take the boys to a nearby fresh produce market to buy peaches. After returning home from the market, the boys headed back out to find the soldiers across the fields. Instead of hiding in the tree, Bunny and his brother mustered up enough courage to approach the young men. The boys took small baskets of peaches with them and sold peaches to the soldiers for five cents each.

As he grew older, my son loved fishing and used to trek on his bike to the banks of the Delaware River, where he fished for catfish. When he returned with the catch, he used to give the fish to his dad. My husband loved it. He buried the fish in his tomato garden as fertilizer.

Bunny loved cars and anything mechanical. He constantly tinkered with tools and technical instruments. I couldn't keep up with all his ingenious ideas. In the early 60s, he drew unusual cars with sleek, pointed fronts, similar to modern-day Corvettes. One time he collected old materials, assembled parts along with four wheels and eventually created a go-cart. His friends joined him and they spent hours going up and down the alley with it. He loved drag racing and watching demolition derbies—all those cars coming together and ramming into each other! It certainly wasn't something I got excited about, yet it fascinated him.

He had a favorite subject in high school, and it was girls. He was a handsome guy who loved the girls and they loved him. He always had plenty of friends and was a natural athlete who excelled in swimming. But dancing was another story. As much as I tried to teach my son to dance, he could never get the hang of it. He always had two left feet!

What Bunny lacked in dancing, he compensated for on drums and percussion. He was always drumming on something. One day he purchased a set of bongos and a snare drum. He kept them hidden in his third floor bedroom, thinking no one knew they were there. My husband and I silently detested them—and so did the rest of the neighborhood. He loved the music of Elvis, Ricky Nelson, and Fabian. But without a doubt, his favorite song was "Wipeout."

Other than girls, the only class at Trenton High School that my son enjoyed was mechanical drawing. His interest led him to a full-time job the summer after his graduation in 1965. He went to work as a draftsman for a company called De Leval Turbine, which made gears for ships. This lucrative job landed my son his own 1963 Corvette Stingray, which he proudly displayed in the driveway.

His steady girlfriend was Carol. Once drafted into the army, he considered marrying her. The issue came up before he left for Vietnam and I had strong opinions against it. My husband was a disabled veteran who served in World War II. The experience of seeing other women whose spouses either didn't return, or returned severely injured, made me convince him that he should wait and marry Carol after his tour in Vietnam. She remained close to our family after Bunny's death, though she eventually married.

My son went to Vietnam feeling strongly that the United States should be there, yet in one letter he wrote from a foxhole, he told me he didn't know if he could ever kill someone. This caused me great concern. At first I didn't know how to reply to his letter, but I wrote back and told him, "Bunny, you do what you have to do when you are in a war."

He was an infantryman and a sharpshooter with the 9th Infantry Division in the Mekong Delta. On May 18, 1967, he was walking on maneuvers, holding his rifle crosswise on the front of his body when a Viet

Cong sniper's bullet ricocheted off the rifle, hitting him in the chest. He died instantly.

My son was laid to rest on Memorial Day. After the military service at Saints Peter & Paul Roman Catholic Church, he was buried there, in the cemetery in Hamilton Township. My husband was a prominent businessman in Trenton, so the community was most supportive. The enormous funeral procession involved over 200 automobiles and it was overwhelming.

Bunny was aware that he was supposed to receive the Silver Star medal for gallantry in action in Vietnam. He died before he received it. In August 1967, I accompanied my husband to his U.S. Army, 7th Armored Division's annual national convention in Milwaukee, Wisconsin. Once again, we found ourselves in the public spotlight. In a televised parade at the veterans war memorial, my husband, now a gold star father, my son, Larry, and I watched as Bunny was posthumously awarded the Silver Star and numerous other medals.

My husband, being sensitive to our loss, was aware of the publicity our family received at such an emotionally stressful time. Knowing that he might pre-decease me, he couldn't endure the thought of Larry and me reliving the funeral process that accompanied Bunny's funeral. He arranged for his body to be donated to Johns Hopkins University Hospital in Baltimore for medical research. His body was cremated and the ashes were buried in Baltimore at the University. Not to inconvenience anyone, a memorial Mass of the Roman Catholic Christian Burial was held the first Saturday after his death in 1980. His headstone was placed at the foot of a grave next to Bunny, where I will eventually be laid to rest eternally in peace next to our son.

The anguish I felt for the loss of Bunny was intensified shortly after he was killed. One day Larry received a letter. I suspected what it was as I opened it. When I read the draft notice, it confirmed my deepest fears. I was overcome with rage. I just stood there ripping the letter to shreds, watching the little pieces float to the floor. I told my friend that a draft notice had come for my second son. She notified the draft board that Larry was now my only remaining son. They never contacted me again.

I struggled to find a reason to go on. I decided to join the American Gold Star Mothers organization, along with another mother who lost her son in Vietnam. I was active for many years and eventually became president of the Trenton chapter and department president for the state of New Jersey. We were an active group.

We spent time volunteering at the VA Hospital, providing recreational activities for veterans who were patients. The men were all ages and from different wars. The older ones were a challenge to work with because they were filled with anger and depression. Many of them had been blinded by explosions and lost their eyesight years before while serving in World War II. I remember one patient who didn't want to socialize or be helped by anyone, even though he needed assistance. He was very resentful when I entered the room one day to begin my volunteer work. He told me in a rather gruff tone, "If you aren't a gold star mother, I don't want to talk to you." When I explained that I was indeed an American Gold Star Mother and had lost my son in Vietnam, his manner changed.

My husband had been injured during World War II, so I became active and served as auxiliary president of the Disabled American Veterans (DAV), Chapter 41, and auxiliary president of the American Legion Post 313 in Hamilton, New Jersey. I was involved in several other organizations and the volunteer work at the VA Hospital helped me feel reconnected to our country. Giving to others helped me deal with Bunny's death.

Another event that helped me work through my grief was seeing the Vietnam Memorial in Washington, D.C. In 1982, 15 years after Bunny's death, I was asked to help usher and greet the thousands of people who attended the opening ceremony. I felt so honored.

****

We moved to a table where Mary shared pictures and articles about her son. The past three decades unfolded before me like a slow motion movie from beginning to end. Her frail hands carefully moved several papers about until she spotted one paper in particular. She continued:

I would like to share this poem with you that my friend, Barbara Rusnak gave me. After my son's death on May 18, 1967, his body arrived home a week later on May 25th and he was buried on Memorial Day, 1967. The Trenton Times printed this poem on Memorial Day, 1987, to honor the twentieth anniversary of Bunny's death. It's my favorite poem and in his honor, I read it every year on May 18th.

The Gold Star Mother
by Barbara Rusnak

The lonely woman comes, bringing flowers for the brave,
A shining tear appears as she looks down at the grave.
The sun softly glistens on the silver in her hair,
Her heart is filled with sorrow as she kneels to say a prayer.

Twenty years ago, her son, heard his duty call
On the field of battle, a brave soldier gave his all.
Now his days will always be without sorrow, without strife
He fought and won our freedom, the price was his life.

The Gold Star is the reminder of a son's outstanding deeds,
But can a Gold Star replace a son's love that every mother needs?
Let's guard our freedom wisely; knowing the price was so dear,
Remember all the Gold Star Mothers, may they never live in fear.

Dedicated to all gold star mothers, especially Mary Korona to honor these women and make more people more aware of the American Gold Star Mothers. I wish the day was here when we could say there are no new gold star mothers, but unfortunately, that is something we may never see.

****

I asked Mary what she would like to tell the world about her son and what she'd tell Bunny now. She paused and then replied:

He was a hero of the United States of America. He saved many lives in Vietnam and spared many loving moms from becoming gold star mothers. He was awarded the Silver Star, but never got to see it. If I could talk to Bunny right now and tell him something, I would say: "Bunny, I love you and I am so proud of you for being the perfect son and soldier. I'm much older now and soon will be resting next to you—dancing the Polka with you and Dad and all the angels in Heaven!"

****

If Mary felt bitterness toward the Vietnam War and the loss of her son, it never showed. Beneath her gentle, courteous demeanor was a witty lady with a twinkle in her eyes. The evening came to a close. I thanked her as Judith and I put on our coats. Caught off guard for an instant, I sensed Bunny's teasing humor as Mary turned to me, grinning. In an eager voice she asked, "So-o-o, when is this book going to be published?"

This dear lady was not going to let the opportunity pass. She knew that her memories of Bunny would now be on paper for generations to read. The despair felt by a mother that her son might be forgotten had turned into hope.

I responded, saying the pen in my hand was moving as fast as it could because her story needed to be told, so others would not forget. Hopefully, I had lifted her spirits. She had certainly lifted mine.

Mary Korona

Private First Class John Dabonka, U.S. Army

New York, New Jersey

B Company, 3rd Battalion, 60th Infantry,
9th Infantry Division

Dinh Tuong Province, Vietnam

KIA: February 2, 1967

Age: 20

"Writing poetry is like a therapy for me.
Instead of paying psychiatrists, I use my pen
and paper. It's cheaper!"

- Virginia Dabonka

American Gold Star Mother Virginia Dabonka contacted me through Judith Young. Though we never met, over the course of five years, Virginia and I became acquainted through correspondence, phone calls and through the poignant war letters from her son, John Dabonka. Upbeat and positive, Virginia wrote poems to express how she felt about the loss of her son. Her poetry reached out to other gold star mothers as well. With Virginia's permission, I have included two of her poems in this chapter and two at the end of the book.

****

John was my oldest son, followed by Joe, who came fifteen months later. Four years after Joe, came Jimmy and then Cathy, my youngest. John graduated from Union Hill High School in 1964. He wanted to enlist in the Navy. He failed one section of the test called the "tool" test, however.

The idea of the Navy suddenly interested his younger brother, Joe, who enlisted at 17. Since John has not passed the naval test, the draft eventually caught up with him. He was inducted in January 1966. I now had two sons serving our country—Joe in the Navy and John in the Army. John was always concerned about our family. After basic training, he was sent to Fort Hood, Texas for Advanced Individual Training (AIT). It was from there that he wrote the following letter:

> Fort Hood, Texas
> Easter Monday, 1966
>
> Hello Mom,
>
> Happy Easter! Have you heard from Joey? Did he make it home for Easter? Does he know where he will be stationed next? How is Cathy? Is Jimmy still bowling? He's not bad, all he needs is practice.
>
> I wrote my girlfriend, Judy, yesterday and told her how much I miss her. The only reason I don't go AWOL is because if I did, we would never be able to have any kind of life together. If it wasn't for her, I really think I would. It is real rough; eight guys still haven't come

back from leave yet, they are AWOL and 10 guys have deserted since we got back. They couldn't take it. One kid went to see the chaplain to complain and the chaplain replied, "I know you are having it real rough; it's because all your Sergeants have just recently come back from combat." They are training us as though we were headed to Vietnam. Don't worry Mom, I'll be all right. Before I know it, it will be time for me to come home, but it seems like a lifetime away. I miss you all so much. If Judy didn't come back to me, I would never make it. Just thinking of her makes me want to do my best. A guy needs something to make him want to try...

I made up my mind so don't worry, I'll be okay. I'm going to volunteer for Vietnam since I have to be here for two years. I might as well go where I think I would be most needed. I'd rather fight than have my son twenty-five years from now fighting for something we didn't finish now. I'd rather die fighting than have my son ever go through what we're going through here. Listen to me talking of dying. I'm too young to die. There's one good thing about going there. They give you a 30 day leave before they send you over. So no matter what happens, I'm sure of coming home first. Please don't worry, I'll be OK.

Today we were shown demonstration of the weapons we will be firing. WOW—too much! They have everything—a rifle that looks like the one Steve McQueen uses in "Wanted Dead or Alive," but it shoots grenades. We have to fire rockets from a sort of Bazooka that can hit a target over a mile away. They have flame throwers, 50 cal. machine guns—name a weapon—they have it. And what's worse, we have to fire them. Don't forget to send me my newspapers (sports especially). Oh yeah, I almost forgot—Happy Birthday Mom! You old sonofagun 43 years young!

Your ever loving son,
yours with all my love.

Johnny

My son had dreams of marrying and eventually having a family. His ideals told him to go to war at the time so his future children would never have to. That letter was heartbreaking for me because he loved his girlfriend, but their relationship didn't work out.

After reading that letter, it felt like he had grown up overnight—one minute I had a silly adolescent on my hands and the next minute he was serving our country. I have one particular memory of him that wasn't funny at the time it happened, but I can look back on it now and laugh.

The boys and I struggled financially as their dad was frequently absent. John and Joe were perhaps 11 or 12 and home on school vacation. I had gone to the dentist to spend money I could ill afford to have a bridge made for my teeth. On the way home I stopped at the local supermarket for groceries. When I arrived at my building, I was told by the neighbors that John and Joe had gotten into trouble with another boy. By this time, my bridge was hurting my gums and I couldn't yell at them the way I wanted to, so I just yanked the bridge out, put it in a napkin and placed it on the top of the groceries. I gathered the boys and shoved them up five flights of stairs, which infuriated me even more. Once in the apartment, John ran in to the bedroom and hid under the bed. I was much younger then. I caught him and gave him a piece of my mind. Joe, on the other hand, thought he would avoid a tongue-lashing and began putting my groceries away—not realizing my bridge had fallen to the bottom of the grocery bag. I never saw the bridge again.

As I reread his letter it hurts to think that John never had the opportunity to have his own children. He was young, and judging from the letter, he was unaware they were training for war. I doubt that he thought long and hard about volunteering for Vietnam because by the time he completed the letter, he was committed.

After eight weeks in Texas and additional training in Fort Riley, Kansas, he came home in November on his long-awaited furlough. He left for Vietnam on December 1, 1966. Cathy, my youngest, was only five and did not accompany us to see him off. My youngest son, Jimmy, and I watched as John left. That was the last time I saw him alive.

He was in Vietnam a short time when his next letter arrived. I'm sure he felt homesick. Despite efforts to remain positive while in combat, I could tell he felt dismay at the living conditions of the Vietnamese.

December 23, 1966

Dear Mom,

Everything is fine. It's better than I thought it would be. We're in a big base camp for a month and it's perfectly safe. We aren't allowed to carry ammo or even keep it in our tents. From all the talk I hear from the guys who have been here for a while, most guys who do get hurt are injured by booby traps because the Viet Cong are very smart at that. It's very seldom that you even see them. They will only fight when they have you outnumbered 3 to 1, otherwise they run.

On base we eat three hot meals a day. Out in the field they fly hot meals to us in the morning and night and we're allowed two canteens of water a day. We get a free beer, soda and cigarettes every other day. On the opposite days you pay for it.

I had a little trouble sleeping last night with all the artillery going off. It was a 175 and has a range of miles but it sounds like a firecracker going off right in my ears. I'm broke but don't send me money. I'll get paid in a few days. You should be receiving $150 in a week. If you need it you can use it, but if not, put it in the bank. I got two envelopes of sports papers.

The people here live like pigs. They don't know

how to use soap, they go to the bathroom where ever they're standing and they don't care who is looking. Kids not even six run up to you and ask for cigarettes. They live in shacks with no doors or curtains—you can see everything inside them. The people are very uneducated. Cathy knows how to spell more than they do. I am really living—I'm glad I have what I have. Our house seems poor to you and maybe you want new things because you think our house doesn't look good but after seeing the way they live, there's no comparison. We are more than millionaires next to them. They have nothing. I can't see how people live like this. It seems funny because in one of your letters you write about the TV going on the blink. At the same time I almost had to laugh. These people don't even have the slightest idea what a TV even is. Right now our big guns are going off and it sounds good knowing it's ours—they don't have any.

By the way, Merry Christmas. Enjoy yourselves and don't worry about me. I'm O.K. and things don't look bad at all. Thanks a million for those sports clippings. It's the first paper we've seen with sports articles and most guys like me are sports fans.

I love you all and I'm sorry I can't be there for the holidays.

Love, Johnny

My son always reassured me that he was safe in Vietnam and not to worry about him. I worried every day. What mother wouldn't? While he was in Vietnam he constantly requested sport clippings of the Yankees. He was a big Yankee fan—to the extent that he wanted to play for them. I still have his application to try out for this major league team.

I started writing poetry in 1958 while watching John play his heart out in a baseball game. I haven't stopped. I write for any and all occasions. I always worked at keeping up my spirits—I do believe that God guides my hands. Poetry is like a therapy for me. Instead of paying psychiatrists, I got therapy through my pen and paper. It was cheaper!

Judy sent my son a "Dear John" letter shortly after he arrived in Vietnam. His plans for their future were gone. He tried to remain cheerful and not dwell on it, but I knew he felt disappointment. It was a rough time for him. He was so busy and exhausted. I wrote this poem and send it to him:

PROUD

It's proud I am of you, my son
It's proud I am of your eyes of blue
And your shock of blond hair
I'm proud of that, too

It's proud I am
when you walk down the street
And proud when a friend
you stop to greet

Yet, prouder still,
 I'll never be
Than that day you said
you were proud of me.

I think as time went on, John began to appreciate our family more. He always showed concern for all of us, including Joe, who was in the Navy.

January 15, 1967

Hi Mom,

I received your letters while I was out in the field and as usual, you made me even more proud of you than

I already am, not to mention how glad I was to receive your mail. Truthfully, I'm really proud of you, even more so as a mother rather than a poet-how about that-you a poet and me a writer, that would be some combination!

Mom, the least of my problems now are girls. That's one of the things I don't have time to worry about. One thing I do not do is worry-it doesn't pay. If I worried about everything over here that there is to worry about, I'd have a nervous breakdown. Things that make other guys scared or shaky don't bother me. I'm fortunate because my Platoon Leader, Lt. Sanderson also keeps a cool head. This man is really sharp. I've already learned a lot about human nature from this man and he's only 23 years old. I can't go wrong following his example. So far in my battalion of about 5,000 men, we have two dead and 23 hurt. The two that died are in another company and they were shot by their own men. The 23 that were hurt was caused by horseplay.

We have been kept pretty busy but it's nothing for you to worry about. I am feeling fine and still in good shape. I count the time until I'll be home. I know I haven't been writing as much as you would like me to, but as I said, I am kept pretty busy and when I do have time off to relax, I like to play pinochle or just lay down to relax and rest.

I still haven't written to anyone except one letter to Joey, which it seems I wrote a long time ago. Please tell him I'm sorry for not writing but I will try to drop a few lines shortly. I'm glad he went back to the ship on my accord. I would feel hurt if he went over the wall. Let's just hope he keeps that idea in mind every time he thinks of taking off. Maybe now that Joe knows I'm sending money home, he will help out too. I hope he keeps his word and sends money home the way he says he will. I'm glad the allotment finally got to you and helps so much. It seems to me I'm glad about everything nowadays.

It takes me a day to write one letter and every chance I have time to write a letter, I'd rather write to you than anyone else. Well, it's about time—I thought you would never send those canned onions to me. I'm waiting for them to arrive. It's good to hear Joe and Dad had a good time. I hope their feelings toward each other are better. Keep on writing about Cathy. I get a big kick out of hearing things about her.
With all my love,
your grateful son,

Johnny

P.S. this is the last letter I'm writing until you send me writing paper and even more important, ENVELOPES—send me a pad of yellow paper.
Thank you very much.

They were issued SP boxes (sundry products) containing personal toiletries such as candy, cigarettes, shaving cream, razors, matches and stationery, but John always lacked enough stationery. He also missed having certain canned fruit and vegetables so I kept him supplied the best I could.

I think my son made a personal assessment of his life and what had made him the man he was. I was touched by his candid remarks of us as parents.

Jan 24, 1967

Hi Mom and all the rest of you lucky people,

Today went pretty easy. We did absolutely nothing all day. I even went swimming in a creek and did it feel good! In the late afternoon we rode a boat out to a bigger type vessel which we have to guard until we are relieved. Don't worry, it's one of the best assignments we've had so far. It's a dry place to sleep. In fact it's pretty easy to sleep on shore and we plan on swimming off the vessel tomorrow. I received your writing paper today as you can tell, thank you. You're a doll.

During some training we took before we came down here to the Delta, two men from my company drowned. They got stuck in the mud and couldn't get out because of all the equipment they had on. What a way to go. It's not bad where I am at. We can buy a can of soda and beer, go swimming and rest—well at least for a while anyway.

The third platoon took out a patrol, or I should say, tried to. They couldn't get more than 50 meters (about 65 feet) past the berm—the mud was up to their waist. There's one good thing—if we can't get to them they can't get to us. I'll write more later. It's my turn to sleep.

I'm writing this letter by moonlight as my soda is being chilled in the water about me. We're finding ways to give Charlie (the Viet Cong) less opportunity to use our things against us. One of his biggest weapons against us is a small can of peanut butter which he makes a beautiful booby trap out of. At first he used to get a lot of it because we GIs won't eat it. It makes us thirsty. We now save all we can get because if we add insect repellent to it, a small can of peanut butter can heat a whole squad's chow. Peanut butter burns and insect repellent burns slow. A can will burn for 10 minutes. More tomorrow. It's my turn to sleep.

Jan 26, 1967

Another page, another day. They all add up. Now all I have to do is keep myself alive until they're all added. So far there's no problem there and I can't see any in the near future. How is Dad? Drinking less I hope at least for your sake. I'm glad to hear that you read him all my letters. I'll let you know something. It really makes me feel good knowing that both of you are proud of me. It's a feeling inside that makes you want to try harder to be good.

Tell Dad I'm pretty proud of him and I'll always be grateful for the help he used to give me when I was small and just learning to play ball. I'll always remember the times he took Joey and me to the park and hit fly balls out to us. There's no doubt in my mind that because of his help that I am what I am today—a fair minded man because of my idea of sportsmanship and my good physical condition. Because of all the sports I played—you name it and I've played it and I'm better than most. I can swim, play football, baseball, basketball, hand ball, volleyball, and bowl, shoot a weapon, run with good speed and throw with a good accurate arm.

All of this I have to be thankful for and from you I have my personality to be thankful for. From you I learned to keep a cool head which a person needs over here. I better end this so I can write Joey. Take care and remember I love you and that goes for Dad, Jim and Cathy too.

I am sending Dad a ten-cent piece for his collection. Also, if I remember, when I leave this place, I will bring you your jar of dirt, O.K.? I just figured it out—I have 302 days left. I heard there is a chance we will be leaving November 23 for good, unless I extend, which I might do.

I don't know yet.

For now, your devoted son,

John

P.S. If you can, mail me a set of TL (wire cutters). I use it for splicing wire and cutting it. One more favor, send me some canned fruit such as peaches, pears, fruit cocktail and so on. It would be a big help.

A week after he wrote that letter, my son was killed. On February 2, 1967 shrapnel from an explosion hit him in the back. After I was notified, I was terribly mad at God for allowing this to happen, and yet found myself walking 15 blocks to the church the next morning, not even worrying about the traffic. It was nine days before John's body was returned to us.

There was no professional counseling at the time. The community was very supportive, though. The greatest support I received during this dark time was from my family and friends. My husband had alcohol and gambling issues—he was of little help. My son, Joe, came home on leave and was a pillar of strength as I tried to deal with John's death and care for James, who was 14 and Cathy, who was five.

I wanted John buried nearby so I could walk to his grave. Joe located a cemetery not far from here. We never heard from John's ex-girlfriend, Judy, again. It hurt me that she didn't attend the funeral, though her family did attend.

After John's funeral, Joe returned to his ship. I think Joe was beginning to feel the impact of John's death when he wrote me the following letter:

Fri. 6 p.m. March 3, 1967

Dear Mom,

I got four beautiful letters this week. It'll be another year before I get all that mail again. I've been staying on the ship lately saving my money I'll never see.

And so, there's not very much to say. I guess things aren't easy for you now. I've got a good memory, Mom, and I remember the things John and me did together a long time ago and the fun we would have had. I don't know about you, but sometimes I'd say to myself, "Hey John, why'd you go do a thing like that for?" We'll not talk about that now. We'll always miss him.

Nice to hear you're going to church. That should help you some. Thanks a million for the money. I don't think I'll need any more.

I've been thinking, I guess I'll stay on this ship. Even before John died, I was thinking about getting small boat duty in Vietnam. But now, I know it would be too much on you. So, I guess I won't. It's a promise. Maybe in some other war. At least that way I'd get off this ship. What's your opinion? I said I won't, so hush. I don't particularly care if anything should happen to me. Live and enjoy yourself. I don't sweat anything here, so you shouldn't worry about anything.

I heard that song a little while ago, "I'll Take Care of Your Cares." I'll let you play it for me. I guess it's an ugly thing for you, Mom, seeing your son gone. It's a strange feeling when you think about it. We pull out tomorrow night. I didn't enjoy saying good bye to you. But soon I'll be home for good. After what's happened I think I'm a much better guy.

As far as John's money is concerned, do what you want with it—buy a house, save it. I really don't want it. Invest it for Cathy or Jimmy in a bank. More later.

I'm back. I suppose it helps when you cry. Try to feel he just went on a long 12 am (mid watch). I'll be thinking of him and everyone back home. But you've got to live too, Mom. Don't cry too much. That's not right. I suppose you'll be crying for a long time to come and I can understand. He can't be replaced, but accept it and just concentrate on Cathy and Jim. I pray you think of the other side of it, instead of crying. Remember—every time I look up at the stars I'll be thinking of you and everyone.

With all my Love Forever,
your Loving Son,

Joe
Write.

We received an insurance policy settlement of ten thousand dollars from my son's death. We were so much in debt at the time; it went mostly to pay off bills. I joined the AGSM organization and met some very nice people through it. I still enjoy receiving their newsletters.

Through the years my son Joe grew depressed. He never got over John's death. After a tragic life of attempted suicides, we lost him to a heart attack at the age of 39.

Years later, I entered a singing contest and met a talented lady, Vera Fagley. I was invited to join the West New York Seniors and we performed in a variety of shows. Vera and I became steadfast friends and now have five gentlemen in our group who play harmonicas. We plan to entertain in nursing homes and Veterans hospitals. God willing, I keep my health. I am so blessed.

I am proud of all my children. I am as devoted to them as they are to me. I love my country now as I did when John was serving. He told me we had to stop communism before it spread too far. My only regret is that my son had not left me any grandchildren. He was too busy fighting a losing battle.

I would like the world to know he was a wonderful young man who helped everyone he could. I am so proud of him and so proud to have been his mom for 20 years.

If I could tell John something, I would say that I love and miss him and think of him daily. I hope he and his brother Joe are now resting in peace.

I wrote the following poem, "My Shining Star," which was published by the New York Times in 1984. Shortly after, a letter arrived on October 1, 1984, from Prescott Bush, brother of then-Vice President George H.W. Bush. Mr. Bush praised my poem as a beautiful tribute to John. He said, "It brought tears to my eyes. It eloquently bespoke the love and gratitude this country feels for those who fought so gallantly under the tough conditions for our freedom." He sent a copy of my poem to his brother, Vice President Bush.

My Shining Star

There's a gold star in my window
In memory of you
It lights my darkest hours
and turns grey skies to blue
There's a new star in the Heavens
that I search for every night
For it stands for faith and courage
and a cause you thought was right
You tried once to explain it to me, my precious
Just why we have to fight this war
and help get justice done
There's a gold star in my window
That will guide me through the years
Even though the road ahead
is dark and wet with tears
So sleep on, my gallant hero,
For even though you lost, you won,
The heart of a grateful nation
You're second best to none.

****

In the back of this book, I have included two other poems that Virginia wrote. I felt as if I had personally known her longer than the few years we corresponded. Sadly, she passed away before I had the opportunity to meet her.

Virginia Dabonka with her two grandkids

Lance Corporal Stephen Boryszewski, U.S.M.C.

West Seneca, New York

H Company, 2nd Battalion, 1st Marine Regiment

Quang Nam Province, Vietnam

Age: 19

"We've always displayed something honoring our son."

- Theresa Boryszewski

When Shirley Popoff invited me to an American Gold Star Mothers meeting in Buffalo, she explained to the members that I was interested in listening to their stories. After the meeting, three members expressed an interest in talking about their experiences. The first to approach me was a petite lady with short, honey-colored, wavy hair. With a soft voice, she told me she would be happy to share her story. This was Theresa Boryszewski, mother of Stephen Boryszewski.

Theresa and her husband raised their three children in a South Buffalo neighborhood called the Valley. After Stephen's graduation from high school, they moved to West Seneca, a nearby suburb. I drove up a quiet, tree-lined street and spotted an American flag in the front window of a small, white, Cape Cod home. Theresa's husband, Stephen Sr., had placed it there in honor of their son after he was killed in Vietnam.

They greeted me warmly and directed me to the kitchen. Stephen's parents went to great lengths for my visit. Over cups of coffee, I noticed boxes, news articles, and photos that covered the table. As I read through their son's letters, one in particular dated "Thanksgiving 1968," stood out. I was struck by this young man's wisdom as he reflected on his brief experience with the war in Southeast Asia. Part of his letter stated:

They've been moving me around quite a bit. Now I'm on a little island out in the rice paddies. It's just an outpost in case we get attacked at the main base, which is 700 meters (about 2200 feet) from here... I can tell you one thing and it's that the war over here is going to last a long time. You know, the U.S. will always be at war because wherever trouble breaks out, the U.S., under the Geneva Convention, made a promise to help. So you see, if I weren't over here now, I might be over here later. I'd be in some other place fighting when it broke out because it may be while the war here is going on or after this. There will always be another place like Viet Nam. Maybe not jungles, not rice patties and not deserts but there will be another war as long as the U.S tries to help other countries....

Theresa began telling me her memories of Stephen.

****

I will remember my oldest son as a loving, considerate, and quiet child who always did what he was asked without a fuss. Whenever he did anything, he did it very well. He would shovel snow to earn extra money and, in turn, he would buy me gifts. At Christmas he always made sure he had gifts for his younger sister Debbie and his little brother Matthew. He was very thoughtful of others.

Stephen's quiet nature was overshadowed by his passion for sports. He was six-feet, and most of all, loved playing basketball at the Boys Club. I still have his basketball trophies upstairs.

Shortly after he began ninth grade at South Park High School in Buffalo, the upper classmen had an initiation day for freshmen. It was nothing harmful, yet I have to laugh as I recall it. One afternoon he was handed a roll of toilet paper at the school. He had to get down on his hands and knees and unroll it all the way down Bolton Street to our house. It was more than just a few blocks, but he took it in stride.

Stephen didn't mind high school, but it didn't interest him either. I think his best times in high school were spent with his three closest friends. One boy was Kevin Kalianski, another was Michael Shimski, and the third was a Native American named Bob Brant. They met in elementary school and remained close friends all through high school.

In June 1967 he graduated from South Park High School. He wasn't sure what he wanted to do, so he began working at National Analine Chemical Company in Buffalo, where he held various positions. It was then that we moved from Buffalo to West Seneca. We were living there about a year when Stephen mentioned the idea of joining the Marine Corps. My husband suggested that he take the Navy entrance test because in the Navy guys have a clean bed and good food. He wanted my son to have a positive experience in the military. Stephen scored high on the test. However, the Navy wasn't accepting recruits. Stephen and another buddy, Rich McCarthy, decided to enlist in the Marines together. They left for basic training at Camp Lejune in May 1968. That day the Navy called to tell him there were openings.

My son came home only once while he was in the Marines, and it was after basic training. I have bittersweet memories of it. Upon his arrival, he immediately informed us that when his furlough was over, he'd be headed to California and then to Vietnam. That's when I started worrying, because the war was at its height and so many young men were getting killed.

My fondest memory of Stephen's furlough was seeing him with his friends. He visited his high school friends in our former Buffalo neighborhood. He wanted to party with those who meant the most to him. He asked us if he could invite Kevin, Michael, and Bob over for one last celebration before he left. We bought them some beer and they partied in our basement. A few days later he departed for California and then Vietnam.

My son was stationed at Da Nang in the province of Quang Nam and was on combat patrol most of the time. His buddy, Rich, served as a cook. If they had time, they briefly spoke to each other as Stephen came in from the field.

While he was in Vietnam, I think Stephen reflected a great deal on the choices he had made in his life. My husband always wanted him to attend college, but the lackluster courses of South Park High School didn't spark his interest. He shared his deepest thoughts with my husband in November 1968 when he wrote an exceptionally long letter saying:

> I felt that my four years of high school were four years of my life thrown away. I know you wanted me to go to college. Sure, I could've made it if I wanted to. But that wasn't what I wanted. All through high school I didn't get very good marks, until my last year when I had something that interested me—print shop and wood shop. They were the two highest marks I had in four years of school...I got to go. I guess I got carried away because I usually write one page and that's it. But it's kind of lonely out here...

Stephen received a military newspaper, the Pacific Stars and Stripes, which covered the war in his area. When the paper came out, he saved pictures and articles and sent them home, indicating where he was in the photo. One article showed him and his comrades carrying babies and evacuating families out of an area from enemy hands. In another letter, he proudly stated:

> As soon as the paper arrives, I'll send you the article. We got a big two-page write up for an operation that we served in. If you hear of Operation Foxtrot, that's the one I was on.

My son realized how much we worried about him. To ease our concern, he sent lots of photos, including one of him and the guys in his unit taking time to relax and play basketball. Beneath the photo he wrote, "See, it isn't all about war." Mud, sandbags, and gray monsoon clouds loomed in the background. In such dismal surroundings, with so little to cheer about, he made the most of a situation where he had no control. I still worried. If my husband had concerns, he wrote Stephen directly and asked questions. My son replied directly to my husband. Occasionally he commented about the skirmishes he was in. In one letter, he told exactly how far away a Vietcong was when Stephen shot and killed him. I think he knew how upset I got, knowing he was in so much combat. He was wounded in the leg once and told my sister about it, yet never said a word to us. He was later awarded the Purple Heart. He faced more than he ever let on.

As the months continued, my son related more about his situation to my husband than to me. In a letter dated January 9, 1969 he wrote:

> I'm walking point now. I had the worst time down here the last four days. We had an operation that was supposed to be two days but it lasted four. It has rained for four days, non-stop. I was in two feet of water, fighting. The whole Battalion went out, but our platoon was the only one that got hit badly. We went out with a twelve-man squad and came back with only four, so you can see I lucked out. I heard that there were 270 confirmed VC dead and only 28 Marines. I was sitting in a big foxhole (filled with water) scared more than I've ever been. You could see the VC trying to sneak up on

us. We opened fire on them, and they were throwing grenades all over the place. That's how most of the guys got hurt. Things have been getting pretty bad down here lately. We just came in last night, and we got another operation tonight at 1:00 a.m. I'm going over to the club to have a few beers and calm my nerves. I haven't been there in a month and a half.

My son had no desire to advance in rank. He was a smart, sensitive kid and I suspect he didn't want the responsibility of making life and death decisions about those close to him. He turned down advancements more than once. Eventually he was forced to move up to the rank of lance corporal, but he would've been content to remain a private.

He was so charitable. I remember him sending his sister, Debbie, a gift and his brother, Matthew, a sweatshirt. One gift in particular I cherish. He ordered a beautiful Bible for us while he was in Vietnam. At first we didn't know what to think when we opened it up. Our first thought was that it was from a sales company trying to promote products to the guys over there, but it wasn't. I'm touched that he thought of it on his own and it was his personal wish for us to have it. It arrived almost on the same day that he died. He shared with his comrades as well. I remember the care packages of snacks I sent him. He was so grateful. His reply was:

I received the package today. But I got an Italian buddy and I asked him if he wanted some pepperoni. He got carried away and saved me about half an inch!

Stephen's biggest wish was for my husband and me to visit New York City. My husband and I think our son's comrades were from there and he was impressed by what they told him about their hometown. Stephen inquired about the best places to visit.

My birthday was approaching and my son wanted to give me something special. In a letter to his father, dated February 6, 1969, he said that he had some money saved in an account and he instructed his dad to withdraw one hundred dollars. He told my husband to buy a new suit and I was to purchase a stylish dress. He instructed us to withdraw another hundred dollars and visit New York City. While there, he told us to enjoy an Italian meal at Mama Leone's on 47th Street and Broadway. After that, he wanted us to go to one of two places, either the Americana on 43rd Street or the Hilton Ballroom on 49th. He closed the letter by saying:

> I never did have the chance to get you and Mom anything decent, Dad. You and Mom took care of me all my life, so I think that both of you would like this a lot. I know you don't like to get dressed up and go out a lot and you say you don't have the time. Well, it's Mom's birthday. I don't want you to take the money and pay bills with it because they can wait. I would appreciate it if you would do this, if not for Mom, then for me. Write soon and have a good time.
>
> Your son,
> Steve

We decided to take the trip when the weather was nicer. Two months later, on April 10, 1969, Stephen came in from patrol as another Marine was getting ready to take his patrol out. The other Marine became sick and couldn't go out, so my son volunteered to replace him. While he was on patrol, a land mine was tripped. He died from shrapnel wounds.

Two Marines appeared at the door to notify us, but they said little about the circumstances surrounding his death. They told us a helicopter was flown out to him as quickly as possible but they had no other details. We were led to believe that Stephen was the only casualty. It was difficult to accept such sketchy details, so we waited for more news. Shortly after, a three-page telegram arrived that was equally disappointing. It upset me terribly, not only because of the lack of information about our son's death, but because it switched abruptly to funeral arrangements and finances.

The telegram stated that Stephen was three miles south of Da Nang in Qua Nan Province on a search and destroy mission when he sustained fragmentation wounds to the body from a hostile explosive device. Our son's remains would be prepared, encased, and shipped at no expense and then accompanied by an escort to either a funeral home or a national cemetery.

It explained that we would be reimbursed in an amount not to exceed five hundred dollars for interment at a private cemetery and two hundred fifty dollars if my son's remains were consigned to a funeral home. If we wished to have services at a funeral parlor and purchase a burial plot, we would be responsible for the additional expenses. The government ended its responsibility there.

Families were compensated ten thousand dollars in the form of an insurance policy, but we incurred higher expenses. To this day, I still feel bewildered when I look back. Many questions remained about his death while we dealt with his burial.

Our wishes were to have a wake and have our son buried in a nearby cemetery. Arlington Cemetery was offered at no cost, but we felt it was too far away. Everyone who knew our son—relatives, neighbors, co-workers, and high school friends—would not have had the chance to pay their respects. With the funds we received from his back pay, plus the military insurance policy, we had a funeral service here for him. He was buried at Holy Cross Cemetery nearby in Lackawanna. I hold out hope that someday one of his comrades will contact us with details surrounding his death.

We had an unusual experience at Stephen's funeral. A young man came up to my husband and introduced himself as a younger brother of the Marine who Stephen had replaced when he went back out with the patrol that day. The young man gave his condolences and went on to say that his brother would eventually stop by and tell us what had transpired. My husband never saw such a nervous wreck in his life. He didn't think to get the young man's name because there were so many people in the funeral parlor and he couldn't stop to talk at the moment. We never saw that young man again.

I believe he and his brother were from Western New York, possibly right here in Buffalo where our kids grew up. I hoped the older brother would stop by and tell us more if he knew anything about Stephen. A priest who was over there at the time contacted us, but he had few details. Other than that, I never heard from anyone who served with my son, though I wish I had.

Stephen's uniforms were returned, but personal items like his watch and class ring from South Park High School were missing. It hurt deeply to think that those items weren't included with his other belongings and shipped home. They mean a great deal to me for sentimental reasons and I would love to have them returned.

The first year without my son was hard, yet my husband was so proud of him. He purchased a beautiful flag decoration to display in the front window for everyone to see, but initially, it was too difficult for me to look at it. He waited a year before putting it in the front window. Since then, we've always displayed something honoring our son.

There were no self-help groups for families who had lost sons in Vietnam. I understand why parents have nervous breakdowns at times like this. The trauma of losing a son was so severe, the only way to get through it was with professional counseling, and even then it was a long time in therapy. For a while after I lost Stephen, I didn't want to go to church. I felt like I couldn't talk to God anymore. Later on, I returned to the church and I anchored my faith in God in order to survive the loss.

I was unaware of the AGSM organization until I attended a ceremony at South Park High School. A plaque had been dedicated in honor of the graduates who were killed in Vietnam. Another mother attending the event had also lost her son, and she asked me if I'd ever thought of joining the organization. I told her I had never heard of it. She offered to take me to a meeting to meet some of the members. I refused at first, saying I didn't want to get involved in anything. She was so kind. She gently suggested that I attend just one meeting to see what it was like. I reluctantly agreed. I was very impressed by the leadership and the wonderful mothers I met. I found the support I needed. I joined the organization and have made many friends since then. Along with the flag that's in our window, we now have an American Gold Star Mothers flag.

Our community has been very supportive of the families. A memorial was built at the West Seneca Town Hall to honor the fallen in Southeast Asia. The Western New York Vietnam Memorial, located along Buffalo's waterfront, lists the 514 local servicemen who sacrificed their lives and my son's name is listed on both memorials.

For years, I experienced many feelings over the loss of my son in Vietnam. I felt differently about the government at that time. I didn't like it. I was very hurt by their decisions and hurt about everything related to the war. To this day I feel that my son never should've gone to Vietnam—that was no war—certainly not for those young guys. It was a foolish decision on the part of the government. And when the boys came home, people spat on them and gave them no recognition whatsoever.

We fulfilled Stephen's wish for us to visit New York City. One autumn after his death, we drove to New York City for dinner and dancing, viewed the Statue of Liberty, and took a carriage ride through Central Park.

****

I asked Theresa what she would like others to know about Stephen and what she would say to him if she could. She paused and with tender emotion, calmly replied:

If I could say anything about him to others, it would be that he was such a good boy. Every time his father needed any help, he was always right there to help out with anything. If I could tell him something, I would tell him, "Stephen, you are such a hero who sacrificed your life for the people of Vietnam, for your country, and for freedom. Stephen, I love you and wish you could be here. Love, Mom."

****

After meeting with Theresa, my journey continued as I met two other American Gold Star Mothers from the Buffalo Chapter.

Theresa and Stephen Boryszewski

Corporal
Henry Patrick Jackowiak,
U.S.M.C.

Angola, New York

Radio Platoon H and S Company,
1st Battalion, 3rd Marines

KIA: September 26, 1967

Quang Nam Province, Vietnam

Age: 21

"When the gold star mothers get together, we know what our common bond is and what brought us together. Nobody lords it over the other one. We all share the same loss. We don't sit and cry. They're a beautiful bunch and we get along well."

- Betty Jackowiak

American Gold Star Mother Betty Jackowiak of the Buffalo Chapter was also introduced to me by Shirley Popoff. I visited Betty on a warm spring day. I drove out Route 5 which parallels Lake Erie, south of Buffalo. As I breezed along the busy highway, I nearly missed the little turnoff on my right that sloped gently down toward the Lake Erie shoreline. I was now off the beaten path, on a narrow road in a community of summer cottages, some of which were winterized. The neatly kept, simple structures were nestled closely together, giving me a feeling that winter on the lake brought neighbors close together—if they chose to remain.

I was about to ring the doorbell, when Betty and her son Marty warmly greeted me. We proceeded to her bright, cheerful kitchen. I sat down at the table and instantly spotted a small framed photo on the kitchen table of a handsome, young Marine with brown eyes and a serious expression on his face. My eyes were drawn to it numerous times during our conversation.

Betty served coffee and we talked about her family. She had a radiating, cheerful smile and a light, graceful lilt in her voice that immediately put me at ease. Meeting her under any other circumstances, I never would've known she had suffered such a personal loss. She glanced at the photo of the Marine and proceeded to speak affectionately of her son, Henry Patrick, known as Rick.

****

Rick was my oldest, followed by Marty and Dennis. Our boys were raised in the neighborhood of South Buffalo called the First Ward. When Rick was in seventh grade, we decided to move to Angola, a small town located 30 minutes from Buffalo, right on the Lake Erie shore. We never regretted it. Growing up near water in the 1960s left great memories of water skiing, boating, and watching Lake Erie sunsets.

My son loved the outdoors in winter as well. He and his dad used to get up on dark, freezing mornings, walk out on barren Lake Erie with a hatchet, and chop a hole in the ice. They would drop a fishing line into the water and wait for a nibble.

Most fishermen tell stories of "the one that got away," but I laugh as I think about the one that would "not" go away. Rick brought fish home for me to fillet and clean. When the fish come out of icy water, they appear dead. One morning he returned with a good-sized perch that warmed up quickly and began to move around, so I put it in the bathtub and turned on the water. I wasn't sure what to do with it—I didn't have the heart to just cut off its head—and neither did Rick or my husband when they saw it swimming around the tub! I phoned my mother and asked for a solution. She calmly replied, "Just let the water out of the tub. It'll die." I took her advice. It was so comical. When I think of my son's ice fishing experiences, that poor perch comes to mind.

Rick's enthusiasm for the outdoors and camping with the Boy Scouts left little room for school. Whenever I became concerned about school, I would think of Sister Grace, Rick's teacher at Our Lady of Perpetual Help Elementary School, who reassured me about him. She always took him under her wing and encouraged him to read, even simple things like comic books. She once told me, "No matter what a child reads, it'll do good just to read." I never forgot that.

My son was fascinated with radios and electronics. As a young boy, I remember him having a crystal radio set in the back bedroom. He attached a wire to it and then ran the wire out the window and up a clothes pole. Once it was connected, he had an aerial that was high enough for reception. Those skills and interests remained with him when he enlisted in the Marines because he eventually taught communications and radio operations.

He was considered a "gear head" who always tinkered with some kind of dune buggy or beach car, like the 1953 Ford that he used to race up and down on the Lake Erie beach. After a while it began to draw the attention of the police as they patrolled the area. They finally reached an agreement that Rick could have the beach for his car rides after Labor Day if he stayed off it during the summer when the residents were at their cottages. It worked out well for the most part. The cottages closed up for the winter and the beach belonged to him.

When we moved here, we bought a tavern on the Lake Erie beach called Lerczak's. Rick worked hard in our family business. At the age of 13, his first job was parking cars. When he was 15, he worked in the basement sorting bottles and stacking beer cases as they were delivered. By the time he turned 18 he had learned how to stack beer behind the bar and how to bar tend—he had the personality to go with it. I still keep in touch with friends from 50 years ago, when we owned the tavern. The other day, a friend of mine shared a memory of my son, which I never knew.

Rick had a friend named Joey who was two years older than him.

Joey had a diabetes problem. Rick was about 15, so Joey was no more than 17. Joey came over one evening to help my son work in the basement of the tavern. At the end of the night, Joey went home that night silly and laughing loudly, which wasn't his nature. Maureen, his mother, became suspicious and questioned her son when he came home, but he insisted that he was just working with Rick in the basement. Joey wasn't supposed to drink alcoholic beverages with his sugar problem. Maureen was fit to be tied and insisted they were drinking, but Joey stuck to his story. My friend knew about the incident because she was with Joey's mother the night he came home from the tavern. I'm astounded that my son, only 15 at the time, was drinking with Joey! But equally astonishing is the fact that I'm just hearing about this for the first time—35 years later!

We had refrigerators behind the bar for the beer, but we didn't have ice machines back then for the soda pop. Large ice blocks were delivered to the basement. There was a huge machine with a crank on it like a coffee grinder and someone had to crank it in order to produce buckets of ice. Rick worked hard chopping the ice, and with the help of a mechanical dumb waiter he hoisted ice and beer upstairs through the elevator shaft. There was a popular beer called Schmidt's Tiger Head Ale during the '60s. I recall hearing how the cases of beer occasionally arrived upstairs feeling rather light. I always thought that Rick and his friends were just chopping up ice for the soda and loading beer on the dumb waiter all the while!

My son graduated from Lake Shore High School in 1964. He was in the graduating class with the country singer and entertainer, Clint Holmes. Their yearbook revealed something about each senior's interests. Beneath Rick's senior portrait was an academic interest and personal philosophy. His interests were listed as, "Business, Drag Racing, and the Marines." The philosophical quote beneath his portrait stated, "If it isn't worth doing, forget it!"

His dream was to become involved in drag racing and eventually become a Marine. For two years after high school my son was involved with cars while working at the nearby Bethlehem Steel plant. During that time, one of his closest friends had just returned from Vietnam. I think he may have persuaded my son to join the Marines because Rick did enlist in 1966. They agreed that when Rick returned from Vietnam, they would build a race car together and compete at Lancaster Speedway, about 30 miles east of here.

After basic training, Rick was sent to Okinawa, Japan, as a communications instructor, a skill that he had been familiar with since childhood. He could have stayed there, but everyone he trained continued to Vietnam. Eventually, he decided to join them. I suspect that his desire to buy a Corvette after returning home influenced his decision to leave his instructor's job in Okinawa for Vietnam. He wrote Marty, saying he wanted a pay increase so he could later purchase a new Corvette. By volunteering for Vietnam, he would receive combat pay, which was more money than he received as an instructor in Okinawa.

Once he had arrived in Vietnam around September 2 he wrote Marty, advising him about school. In one of his last letters, Rick advised Marty to stay in school and never abandon his education. Marty had four years of college ahead of him and was enrolled in the Army ROTC program at the time.

Rick was a radioman in Vietnam—they were always a target for the North Vietnamese. If the enemy could eliminate the radioman, there was a better chance of disrupting communication among American troops. My son was not in country long. Three weeks after arriving, he was killed by enemy fire on September 26, 1967.

We endured his death, but certain painful moments still surfaced afterwards. Three years later in May 1970, the Kent State shootings created protests across the country. It disturbed me to think my son fought in Vietnam, in the service of our country, while his younger brother, Marty, later faced anti-war protestors on campus. Marty mentioned that a professor approached him and asked why he was going to class when there was a strike on campus against the Vietnam War. The professor asked my son how he could go to class if he cared about what was happening to our country. Rick had inspired Marty to stay in school and complete his degree. It was the government insurance policy for Rick's service to our country that helped pay for Marty's education.

I didn't experience confrontational moments as Marty did. However, I had one unusual experience a few years later that I will always remember. I was at a picnic when a friend of Rick's, who had also served in Vietnam, approached me. His name was Gary and he asked me if I still had Rick's letters from Vietnam. I thought perhaps he wanted to read them and replied that, indeed, I still had all of them. Yet his response shocked me when he said, "Do yourself a favor and burn them. I don't want you to read those and be crying. I don't want you to feel bad. You should get rid of those."

I thought—what an attitude! Some guys who were over there can't even say a word about it.

I like to talk about my son. It's not healthy to hide it or keep it inside. I was able to deal with my grief and I was glad to be a member of the AGSM organization. It is such a wonderful group for mothers. I joined in 1990. When we get together we know what our common bond is and what brought us together. Nobody lords it over the other one. We all share the same loss. We don't sit and cry. They're a beautiful bunch and we get along well.

I regret that other mothers refused to join, but I certainly understand that perhaps the organization was too painful a reminder of their loss. On the other hand, the American Gold Star Mothers have done a world of good for those mothers who have joined. We work to perpetuate the memory of our sons. In turn, the community acknowledges our loss. We have a beautiful parade in our town on Memorial Day and all American Gold Star Mothers are included in it. The mothers have often been in the first car, usually a convertible, and it follows right behind the color guard at the beginning of the parade. I feel this is an important event since it recognizes the American Gold Star Mothers and their sacrifices.

I remember one lady from my town who chose not to become a member. Her son was killed just four months after my son, Rick. I can't help but think that maybe if she had joined, it would have been to her benefit. Our sons knew each other. They weren't real close friends, yet they were buddies. I thought of that mother on Memorial Day, as I was honored in the town parade. All I could think was that while I was being recognized by the citizens for my loss, this other lady refused to join.

In Rick's honor, the Vietnam veterans established the Henry Patrick Jackowiak American Legion Post. Due to the fact that the members had other commitments and responsibilities, it remained open for about three years, but then closed. The charter was surrendered due to the declining enrollment. It was too bad they couldn't keep the post open, but we were presented with a huge, elegant dress flag from the post when it closed. We felt so proud. I still take it out on special occasions and hang it on my clothesline to be displayed.

I feel deep respect for the American flag. Just before Rick left to go overseas, he phoned home, telling me that he was a flag bearer for the color guard in a parade. I recall his comment to me. "Oh, Mom! I was so proud. My heart just swelled as I carried that American flag!"

Even seeing an American flag in a parade makes me proud. Our country's history is represented in that flag. It has affected my life and the direction my life took as a result.

My son is buried in Holy Cross Cemetery in Lackawanna close to Lake Erie where he grew up and attended school, and not far from the steel plant where he worked before leaving for Vietnam. I could've elected to have him buried in Arlington National Cemetery, but I chose not to do that. I picked someplace close to home, close to me and, close to my heart.

He's never far from my thoughts. On the kitchen table is the little framed picture of him in his Marine fatigues. It remains there and greets me every morning. Others notice it when they come by to visit or when friends stop in for a cup of coffee. I gaze at it often during the day and smile. I can reach out, touch it, and tell him, I love you, and I miss you.

****

Betty and her husband sold their tavern after Rick's death. Later, it became well known to Western New Yorkers as the famous "Mickey Rats" bar on Lake Erie. A special friendship developed after I visited Betty and her son, Marty. She remembers me every year with a Christmas card.

Betty Jackowiak

Private First Class Richard Allen (Buddy) Knaus, U.S. Army

Cheektowaga, New York

B Battery, 2nd Battalion, 19th Artillery,
1st Cavalry Division

Binh Dinh, Vietnam

KIA: December 27, 1966

Age 21

"We have the best country in the world and I am ever
so grateful that we live here."

- Alice Knaus

American Gold Star Mother Alice Knaus was the third member of the Buffalo Chapter whom I had the pleasure to meet. When Alice entered a room, other mothers couldn't help being drawn to this little, matronly lady with a cheerful spirit. Every mother kept her ears open, expecting Alice to ignite peals of laughter with her witty jokes about blondes, men, or marriage. Her sense of humor was a gift she shared with everyone she knew. Her presence surely lifted the spirits of other mothers in their darkest moments or when the organization gathered for various events.

Alice lived with her youngest son, Howard, and his wife, Dawn. They lived minutes from my house. Warmly greeting me at the back door, they led me to their small, cozy kitchen. The four of us sat down at the kitchen table, where photos and news articles were spread out for me to read. We looked over letters from her son, Buddy, while he was in Vietnam. One in particular caught my eye. It was his last letter to Alice. It read:

****

16 December '66

Dear Mom,

I received your letter of 8 Dec. yesterday and your Christmas package about five days ago. Thank you very much. I also received a couple of packages from Grandma and one from the Sattlers Social Club with a Christmas card. Would you thank Grandma and your boss for me? I'm out on an operation right now. We left base camp the 12th. The operation's supposed to last sixty days. We left base camp by convoy and went to Hannon Airstrip and then lifted out by Chinook to where we are now, in Bong Son.

I got myself a dog about two days before we moved out. I bought him from a Vietnamese barber in town for $1.00. He's about seven weeks old, I call him Chief. I brought him out on the operation with me. It's been raining off and on. The dog hasn't been doing too much running around because the mud is up to his belly. He sleeps in my pup tent with me on my towel.

We've been real busy since we've been in the position filling sand bags and putting them around the gun area and building bunkers. One of the guys in my gun section got a two-foot aluminum Christmas tree in the mail and some small ornaments. I guess we'll set it up a couple days before Christmas.

I'm going to have to close because I haven't mailed out any Christmas cards yet and I haven't much time. I've been doing just fine and I hope everyone back home is also. There isn't anything I could get anyone for Christmas over here, so I'm sending money so everyone can get what they want. I guess that's about it, Merry Christmas, Mom, Dad, Robert, Joan and Howie.

Love, Bud

Howard listened and Dawn made copies of letters and news articles for me while Alice softly recalled her son.

****

My third son was baptized Richard Allen Knaus, but we always called him Bud or Buddy. Robert and Harold were his two older brothers. Buddy was in the middle, followed by both a younger sister, Joan, and a brother, Howard.

Buddy was a good-natured, generous kid who shared everything he had with friends or anyone in need. He always seemed to connect with those less fortunate. His final moments were described in a book about Vietnam battles. He died while trying to protect a comrade.

As a little boy, Buddy had a witty sense of humor and entertained us nightly at the dinner table. We always gathered for dinner at precisely five-thirty. When my husband, Ben, came home, he discussed work and our five kids usually talked about school or events. I talked about calls received from family members or about my day. But Buddy's sense of humor at the table spilled over to any topic. His humor never appealed to his older brothers. Perhaps it was their age difference—maybe his brothers had a more sophisticated humor. I remember one evening at dinner Buddy called his older, serious brother "Stone Face," which made us laugh even more. The nickname stuck, cementing his role as a comedian.

Buddy had a deep concern for the welfare of animals. As I read through his last letter about acquiring a puppy, memories returned of animals he had brought home when he was young. One snowy day I found a cigar box on the floor by the heat register in the living room. I opened it up and sleeping on the top of some cotton pieces were these tiny, pink mice! They were so young, their eyes had not opened yet and they had no fur on their bodies. Buddy had found them in the field by our house. He said it was so cold, he feared they would freeze to death so he brought them home to care for them. He wanted to keep them but I immediately squelched that idea. We could've had quite a menagerie if he had kept all the animals he brought home.

As he got older, my son enjoyed hunting or fishing with his dad and brothers. Once, they came across an injured baby raccoon and brought it home. After cleaning out the wound, they called the zoo to find out how to feed and care for it. The raccoon was so small that Buddy fed it formula from a baby bottle and kept it warm. He named it Rudy. If we went somewhere, like on a family picnic, Bud placed him in a box and brought him along—with a hot water bottle and formula.

When Buddy was about 12, he went to the town park on a summer day with Robert and Harold. He spotted an enormous turtle and brought it home. I have no idea how he did it. My husband was shocked and wouldn't let the kids go near it. They were unaware it was a snapping turtle. It was so strong that it grabbed on to a broomstick handle as we tried to move it. It would have seriously hurt the kids so we had to tell Bud he couldn't keep it. They boxed up the turtle and Ben drove the boys to the zoo. Bud lugged it from one building to another, asking various caretakers if they would take it, but they refused. The box was getting heavy and he was growing tired. Eventually, they found a caretaker who took it off their hands. Bud came home happy, but not as happy as I was to see it gone.

My son's love for art was easier to deal with than his passion for animals. He was five when I recognized his artistic ability so I always encouraged him to develop that talent and fortunately he excelled in high school. Years later, his artistic endeavors proved to be a gift to me as I look back on his art work.

He was about 14 when the Thruway Plaza opened nearby. To attract the public, the plaza held various promotions. One was a Native American Village exhibit with dancers. Chief John Big Tree from the Onondaga Reservation in Syracuse was going to be there. If I remember correctly, Chief John Big Tree was one of three men who had posed for the Indian Head Nickel in 1912. Knowing my son could draw well, I was so excited. "Oh, Bud, look!" I told him, The Indian Chief is going to be at the plaza! Take this Indian Head Nickel and some paper, go upstairs, and draw a picture of him. Then go to the plaza and have him sign it!"

He begged. "Ma, please! Oh God, no!" He protested—but being the good kid that he was, he went upstairs and created a beautiful drawing, based on the Indian Head Nickel. When he approached Chief John, Buddy refused to ask him to sign it.

"My mother would like you to autograph this, please," he said. The Chief signed it. I treasure the memory of that event as well as the art work. I still have that very nickel and I later framed his drawing.

Bud's greatest strength was his artistic ability. His high school teacher, Mr. Joseph Granditz, influenced him greatly and helped develop his talent. Bud was a natural at drawing and painting by the time he reached Advanced Art. He signed and dated ceramic vases after creating them on a pottery wheel. He was about 16 when I realized his artwork was worthy of being displayed.

Our town had an annual art show in the park, so once again I insisted that he take one particular vase down to the art show and submit it for judging. I can still hear his protests when I brought up the idea. "Ma, I ain't sitting down there with a stupid vase!"

I tried to gently encourage him. "Go down to the competition, Buddy. You might win something!"

"Ma—I'm not going!" he replied.

Fortunately, his dad was present and spoke up. "Bud, do as your mother says." Bud grudgingly took the vase and entered it in the exhibition for judging. He was awarded a ribbon—and a prize of $10.

As the show came to a close, the student artwork was put up for sale and someone purchased the vase. We wondered if it was Mr. Granditz because many years later, the vase came back to me. We think that after Mr. Granditz passed away around 1990, his family donated Buddy's vase to local AMVET Buddy Knaus Post #14, named in honor of my son. The post returned it to me. I never imagined I would see that vase again, and I was so grateful to have it.

Bud's love for art extended to others in our community who benefited as a result. He expressed an interest in becoming an art teacher. We lacked the financial resources for his education, so he never had the opportunity to attend college. After his death, the AMVET Post established an art scholarship in Bud's memory. It was awarded every year to a promising art student from Cheektowaga High School from where my son graduated June 1964.

Buddy went to work at Super Duper, a local supermarket, for a year. He was training for the position of Assistant Manager when his draft notice arrived. He was inducted October 29, 1965, along with his close friend, Wayne. Their Army experiences were parallel almost to the end. They were drafted at the same time, their serial numbers were identical except for the last digit, and they were stationed together in Vietnam. I remember seeing Bud leave for Basic Training. Wayne's family and ours stood at the train station as we watched them depart for Fort Dix, New Jersey. We had no idea what their future held.

After basic training in December, Bud went directly to Fort Sill, Oklahoma, for field artillery training through March 1966, followed by training as a paratrooper at Fort Benning, Georgia. His only furlough was April, 1966, just before leaving for Vietnam and I have such vivid memories of it.

Bud never mentioned he was leaving for Vietnam. One afternoon, I took his laundry downstairs to wash. As I began sorting it, I suddenly spotted green underwear. Green underwear? Why would they have green underwear? I then realized they were sending him to Vietnam. Their clothes had been issued to them before the furlough.

We always attended Sunday church services together. Being home on furlough was no exception. "You have to go to church, Bud," I told him. I can still recall his protest,

"Aw, Ma, please! I just got home!"

"You've got to go to church, Bud. Those are the rules." He gave in and went with us.

Bud landed in Vietnam on May 3, 1966. He and his friend, Wayne, were stationed at An Khe Base, but had different duties. Wayne was a machine gunner on helicopters and was flown out to assist his comrades when the need arose. My son was an Infantryman in artillery and operated 175 mm Howitzers. He often spent one or two months in remote locations, establishing and defending an outpost if it was attacked by the North Vietnamese.

He said little about his work during those eight months. By Christmas 1966, he seemed homesick. It was in his last letter that he mentioned the two-foot aluminum Christmas tree with ornaments. I still think of the fact that while he was in combat, he never lost his generous spirit and love for us.

Included in the last letter was his family Christmas gift. He sent my husband and me 75 dollars each, along with 10 dollars for each brother and his sister. He was always so generous. Even as a young news carrier for the Buffalo Evening News, Bud helped his older brothers work a route of 300 customers. He came home and always gave his weekly tip money to me.

It must have been lonely, facing two months of rain at a remote outpost called Landing Zone Bird—LZ Bird. Given those conditions, I can see why he brought a puppy along. That was when he wrote his final letter dated December 16, 1966. On December 27, 1966 in the middle of the night, Bud's outpost was overrun by North Vietnamese solders. My son lost his life in the attack.

When I was notified, I could not believe it. My Buddy? Killed in Vietnam? It can't be so. Not my son, Buddy! Everyone was so concerned about us—our church, family, and neighbors. The entire community supported us. I received many letters on behalf of Bud's heroic efforts in Vietnam. I think citizens recognized the sacrifices our servicemen made. A Memorial Day service is held every year at the Cheektowaga Town Hall, honoring the fallen with a color guard presentation and a prayer.

My son's body was shipped home on New Year's Day, 1967. I wanted him to be buried with his grandfather and uncles at the Buffalo Cemetery on Harlem Road in Cheektowaga. A plaque was placed there honoring him for his service. My entire family has great faith in God and that was where we got our strength.

Four months after Bud's death, his friend Wayne returned from Vietnam. He came directly from the airport to see me. We both grieved.

Wayne said he and Buddy had spent a few moments together at An Khe Base before Buddy was airlifted out to Bong Son. That was the last time Wayne saw Bud. Wayne remained behind at An Khe Base when, on December 27, the alarm went off in the middle of the night signaling a need for reinforcements. Unbeknown to Wayne they were headed to Bud's outpost. Wayne then learned that Buddy had lost his life.

I joined American Gold Star Mothers Chapter 26 shortly after Bud's death. It's such a good organization. It was there for me in the time of my loss. I have made friends with many mothers and we still keep in touch. The VA Hospital is close by. As an American Gold Star Mother, I have found it comforting to volunteer there and assist the veterans.

I never saw The Wall in Washington, D.C., but friends of mine went. They brought back a rubbing of Bud's name which I cherish. I had the opportunity to view The Moving Wall several years ago and again when it appeared at the cemetery where Bud is buried. I do not feel differently about our country after losing my son. We have the best country in the world and I am ever so grateful that we live here.

I had few details about my son's death until a book came out titled, *The Battle For Bird* [S.L.A. Marshall, New York: Warner Books, 1989. p. 39.] Marshall served in three wars during his military career. He served with Buddy in Vietnam and gave a detailed account of his death. I was stunned by what I learned about my son. Bud had befriended Donald Lederhaus, a soldier in his unit:

> When the fight began, several of the crew had ducked into a bunker under the mortar pounding. Next, Pfc. Donald Leaderhaus had frozen on the gun and would not budge. His close buddy, Pfc. Bud Knaus, had stayed there to try to protect him. Johnson came up just in time to see what was happening. Several enemy skirmishers had popped over the parapet. Leaderhaus and Knaus were shot dead by bullets; one got it in the head and the other in the chest. Knaus had died with his body across that of his friend, trying to shield him, a hero unrewarded. Johnson drove the skirmishers off with the rifle fire and stayed on with the two dead men.

My son died trying to shield his friend. At the Vietnam Veterans Memorial Wall in Washington, the position of my son's name in relation to that of his friend, Donald Lederhaus, is noteworthy. Buddy's name is on Panel 13E Line 084, again covering his friend, Donald Lederhaus, whose name is directly beneath Bud's on Panel 13E Line 085.

If I could tell this nation one thing about my son, it would be that he gave his life for a country that he was so proud he could serve. Bud loved people from an early age and he later gave his life trying to protect a comrade. If I could tell Bud something, I would say, "Bud, we thank God for giving you to us for 21 wonderful years. We miss you and we remember your kind, loving ways. And we miss you at the nightly dinner table when you kept us laughing."

****

Buddy must have acquired his sense of humor and love for people from Alice. I had the pleasure of getting to know Buddy's brothers and sister throughout the years. Alice's stories and jokes kept her family in good spirits and she also made me feel most welcome when I visited her.

Alice Knaus

Specialist 4
Cary Dwayne Miller,
U.S. Army

Richmond, Indiana

HHC 4th Battalion, 23rd Infantry,
25th Infantry Division

Tay Ninh Province, Vietnam

KIA: October 6, 1969

Age: 20

"I continued to search for answers about my son's
death. I had no answers until 14 years later."

- Marjorie Miller

I wanted to hear more stories from other gold star mothers so I placed an announcement in the Locators column of the Vietnam Veterans of America Newspaper, asking if any readers knew of gold star mothers who were willing to share their stories. Shortly after, a letter arrived from Richmond, Indiana that read:

> *Dear Linda,*
>
> *I want to wish you good luck on your book. Here are a couple of families [unrelated] whose sons were killed over there. They are members of our Vietnam Veterans Chapter 777. We also have some sisters who belong, since their brothers were killed there, too.*
>
> *Butch Mullen*

Butch's letter directed me to two American Gold Star Mothers from Indiana; Marge Miller from Richmond and Edith Miller from Fountain City. Neither had ever heard of the American Gold Star Mothers organization. They first heard about the organization from me when we met in 2001. For years, Marge Miller and Edith Miller provided support to each other while searching for details about their sons' deaths.

A trip to Indiana gave me the chance to meet these two friendly ladies who were eager to talk about their sons. Summer had just begun and the eight-hour drive from Buffalo through the sweltering Midwest heat to Indiana was long, but worth it.

Marge, mother of Cary Miller, was a practical lady with common sense and a great deal of love in her heart. She and her only daughter, Kathy Kirtley, greeted me warmly. Marge invited me into her small, well-kept, three-bedroom home. In the softly lit, air-conditioned colonial-style living room, Marge introduced me to her husband, Jess, and explained the purpose of my visit to him. Jess, who has since passed away, was a frail man suffering from Alzheimer's disease. He had been a master mechanic who shared his mechanical knowledge and building skills with his son. In 1962 they had built this house together. Marge, Kathy, and I sat at her round colonial kitchen table and talked about her experiences. Linda Ritter, who had been Cary's fiancée, joined us later in the afternoon.

****

I think that my son's greatest quality was his good nature. He was a happy, easygoing kid from day one and he never lost that. Cary had close, fun-loving friends. As a teenager, he worked hard for what he wanted, often juggling a job with sports. As a kid, he began racing competitively at an indoor roller rink. He felt comfortable only if I watched him skate for recreational purposes with his friends on weekends. That was my only opportunity; he wouldn't allow me to watch him compete. He always said, "Maw, it makes me nervous when you watch me compete. Come back and pick me up."

He loved football and played throughout high school. His solid, six-foot, 185-pound frame afforded him the opportunity to be a defensive tackle. I used to laugh and tell him, "There's no way I'm going to let you fall on me or you'd kill me!"

He never minded school, but occasionally enjoyed cutting class. When fourth hour class ended, students ate in the cafeteria or went out for lunch. His sister, Kathy, who was two years younger, attended the same school, and worked in the library that overlooked the entrance, so she could see the kids leaving. As she watched Cary leave with his friends, she knew whether he intended to cut out for the day or just return late. She'd call out, "I'm telling Maw on you!"

Most of the time the kids referred to me as "Maw" rather than "Mom" and that's their dad's fault because when the kids went to Jess for something, his reply was always, "Go ask your Maw."

We worked hard to provide for our son and daughter. When Cary got his license, he was allowed to drive to school, but he had to take Kathy with him. That was the last thing in the world he wanted. Every morning as he prepared to leave, he used to sit in the car, honking the horn and yelling, "Come on if you're riding with us!" Out the door she flew, climbing into the back seat and ever so proud to be with him. From there, they'd head over to pick up Cary's best friend, Andy.

Everything was fine until Cary started up the road that took them to the high school. He didn't want to be seen with his younger sister, so he used to order her to hide, saying, "You stay down in that back seat and don't you pop your head up!" As they approached the school, he drove with one hand on the steering wheel and the other trying to hold Kathy's head down in the back seat. Andy sat up front, reaching back in an attempt to help him. Kathy dodged their hands, weaving her head back and forth to peek out the window. Though she was proud to be seen with them, he dreaded that. I remember hearing about those rides.

My son was a handsome kid and so popular with the girls. He never failed to get a response from Kathy when he teased her, saying, "I am so handsome!" Kathy always retorted, "You're so conceited, too!"

He loved cars and motorcycles. In his senior year he held two jobs in order to pay for his vehicles. We agreed to pay for his insurance. His first car was a blue 1956 Ford that my husband, Jess, helped him repair. Cary was mechanically inclined, but not to the extent that his dad was. Jess was always there to oversee the mechanical aspects. Once, when winter was setting in, the radiator on Cary's car needed to be replaced. Carey procrastinated for some time and it drove my husband crazy. Cary still hadn't fixed it. When Jess looked at the car one day, he turned to me and said emphatically, "I'm not doing that job."

I agreed with him and replied, "Let him do it himself." Shortly after, Cary came in with his friend, Dennis. I fixed them something to eat, then they left in Dennis' car; supposedly to get another part for the radiator. The house grew quiet and the next thing I noticed, Jess was gone. I went outside looking for him. Sure enough, he was working on the radiator. He turned to me saying, "Well, he'll never get it back together properly." In the end, my husband relented and fixed it himself.

I also have memories of Cary's Triumph motorcycle. He only had it a few weeks when my younger brother, Randle, met up with Cary on Route 27, the main drag in downtown Richmond. My brother was five years younger than me, so he was no kid himself. He pulled up in his car and challenged Cary on his motorcycle to a drag race through, of all places, the hospital zone. A few minutes later the police picked both of them up. Cary lost his license for 15 days.

I always expected honesty from my kids. Cary was never one to try covering his mistakes, so when I heard about it, I yelled at him, exclaiming "Cary! Don't you know better than to do that?!"

His only reply was, "Well, we were drag racing!"

Jess, who normally left all the discipline up to me, quietly stepped in and announced, "I'm going to take the motorcycle around."

Shocked that his father would entertain the thought, Cary replied,

"No, you're not!" Cary never wanted anyone touching his motorcycle. But there was nothing he could do about it. For 15 days, my husband rode the motorcycle around on our property and drove our son crazy. Other than the speeding ticket, the biggest difference I had with Cary was over the loud dual muffler pipes on his motorcycle. The disagreement surfaced while he had lost his license. I told him he had a week to tone the muffler down or he was not going to drive it when the restriction was lifted. He challenged me, saying, "What makes you think I can't drive it?"

"The insurance is in your dad's name so I'll pull the license and cancel the insurance on it," I replied. "It's your choice." I wasn't going to allow him to increase our insurance. He promised he'd do something about it when he could find the time and eventually he did. However, I suspect that once he got out on a country road, he found a way to open them up, making a lot of noise when he wasn't around our house! Truthfully, he was not real hard to handle. If I saw a problem, I always got after him before anyone got hurt. You have to teach your kids. If you don't teach them, they don't learn.

My son graduated from Richmond High School in 1967 and began studying IBM communications in Louisville, Kentucky. I wanted him to attend college in Indianapolis because it was closer to home and my mother lived there, but he insisted on going to Kentucky. He wasn't there long when he decided to transfer to Indianapolis. While transferring there, he was dropped as a matriculated student in Kentucky. This instantly signaled a change in his deferment status with the draft board. In a short, two-week period between transferring schools, he became eligible for the draft.

He was unaware of it when he started school in Indianapolis. He was studying electronics there when his draft notice arrived. By then it was too late and he couldn't do anything about it. He was given the option of enlisting in the Army or the Marines. He chose the Army.

In addition to basic training at Fort Benning, Georgia, he was stationed in New Jersey and Alabama. His warfare training included exposure to noxious gases which got into his lungs, causing pneumonia. There was no permanent damage, but it alarmed me when he called home. I told him he needed to get treatment at the infirmary, but he refused. "If I go down there, they'll put me in the hospital, and I'll have to start the training all over again. I don't want to go through that." He completed the training and was sent to Fort Hood, Texas. It was there that he received his orders to go to Vietnam.

He came home for a month furlough in March 1969. On March 31 we took him to the airport where he left for California. The next day he called home, but we could only talk for a few minutes. I wanted to hear from him again. "Cary if you get a chance, call again before you leave," I told him.

"Maw, I'm not calling again," he replied.

"Call once more, even if you only have a second to talk," I said. I think it was too hard for him emotionally to call. That was the last time I spoke with my son. He left on April 2 for Vietnam. He was there for six months and four days when he was killed on October 6, 1969.

When he was drafted I knew deep inside that he was going to Vietnam before anything was ever mentioned. When I told my mother I didn't feel good about this, she tried to reassure me. "You're just worried," she said.

"No, that's not it," I told her. I felt that he wasn't going to come back alive. It's not a good feeling. Yet, it's almost better to admit it. You expect it. When I expressed this concern to a girl I worked with, she also said I was just worried about him. She didn't get what I was saying. Every day at work I waited for that phone call. Cary expressed the same sentiment. Just before leaving for Vietnam, he hinted to his fiancée's brother that he didn't think he was going to return home.

That uneasy feeling returned in September during Labor Day weekend. Jess and I took our boat and went camping at St. Mary's Lake near Salina, Ohio. While there, I had a vivid dream. I dreamt that I got home from work, and Kathy was waiting for me.

"Maw, you've got to read this letter. I don't want to give it to you, but you've got to read it." She handed me the letter. *We are informing you that your son has been killed in Vietnam.* I awoke from the dream so upset. I could never get rid of it. One month later, in October, we were notified.

Cary's close friend from high school, Dennis Landreth, was also serving in Vietnam at the time. He was stationed about 35 miles from Cary. They never had the opportunity to get together while there, though. Knowing they were close friends, my husband and I considered having Dennis escort our son's body home, but it would've taken roughly ten days to process the orders. It was best that we didn't request it because I think it would have been extremely difficult for Dennis' mother to see her son return to Vietnam for a second time, so we decided against it.

My son is buried in Glen Haven Cemetery near Boston, Indiana. He could've been buried in Arlington but I wanted him close to home. I'm very familiar with losses from the Vietnam War because I lost five relatives there. My husband's great nephew and namesake, Jessie Allen, was the first relative killed in Vietnam while serving his second tour there in August 1967. Then my cousin Ken Allen from Berea, Kentucky was killed in December 1967. My cousin Marge lost her son Michael David Hale in August 1968, followed by her stepson, Stanley Clingler, in March 1969. This was followed by Cary's death in October 1969.

I feel fortunate that Cary sent me photos of Vietnam. He took many pictures of the Vietnamese children, a monkey and a dog that the guys adopted as a pet. About three weeks before he was killed, I received three beautiful photo albums. He never said much about his duties, but judging from the pictures of him and his friends, I think his work involved tanks and clearing tunnels of enemies with a powerful gun called a flamethrower. My son experienced a great deal in the six months he was in Vietnam. I kept all his letters. One in particular was touching. He confided:

> I'm fine and homesick. All day yesterday we waded through rice paddies up to our waist and the Vietnamese fertilize them with human waste.

I don't think most people give serious thought to what these men went through. They had to drink from ponds and rivers when fresh water wasn't flown in. They used a great deal of pre-sweetened Kool-Aid to make the local water palatable. In one letter, he asked me to send him some juice. Cary never drank tomato juice, but when I went to buy him his favorite kind, nothing was available except tomato, so I sent it to him. "Mom, that tomato juice tasted so good," he wrote then.

We take so much for granted here at home. When they were out on patrol for days at a time, they ate nothing but C-Rations and they always had wet feet—it was impossible to keep them dry. He always asked for socks. At one point he said he couldn't wait to get back home to take a hot shower, eat a hot meal, and sleep on dry sheets because he hadn't showered in 21 days. In one of his last letters, he wrote us saying he was about to be moved. He also tried to keep an upbeat spirit as he humorously reflected on my advice, saying:

> I can't write too well. If I had listened to you and studied like I should have in school, I could have written better. They are going to take me out of the infantry Unit and sending me to Cu Chi where I will be working in the 725th Motor Pool. It is a safer job and I won't be out in the field anymore or eating C-Rations. I'll be at a base and it'll be nice. I won't know how to act! I'll be moving in a week or so.

My son considered himself lucky. Some of his comrades had to stay out on the front line the entire time they were in Vietnam.

I was at work when two men in uniform came to notify me. We later received a telegram informing us that Cary had been in a military vehicle when he received chest fragmentation wounds and died instantly. Nothing more was said. I wanted to know more details so I wrote the captain of his unit who replied shortly after. He said that a small memorial service had been held for my son and those who served with him had attended. Nothing else was mentioned. He enclosed names and addresses of a few soldiers that Cary knew.

Cary's fiancée, Linda, and I wrote them, asking if they could provide any information. In 1970, almost a year to the day that Cary died, Linda received a letter from Peter Bordinelli who had served with my son. Peter's leg was severely wounded, and he was evacuated by helicopter in the same attack that took Cary's life. Peter was sent to Japan for a few months and then to the United States where he was still recuperating when Linda's letter caught up with him. He had lost contact with the men in his unit after being wounded, so he was unaware that Cary had been killed. The first that he heard of the tragedy was when Linda wrote him, inquiring about Cary. She was searching for answers about Cary's death, but instead, she had the misfortune of informing Peter about my son.

After Peter's reply, Jess and I visited him in Fort Pierce, Florida. We spent two hours with him and learned more. Cary and the others were in a tank or an armored personnel carrier, guarding a road in Tay Ninh. Peter had just gone down inside the tank to do something when it either tripped a wire or was hit by a rocket. He went up above and attempted to get Cary down off the top of it, when the tank was hit a second time. At that moment Peter's left leg was seriously injured. He couldn't give us any more information than that.

Jess and I traveled over a thousand miles seeking answers about Cary. We were most grateful, but I still had other questions. I continued to search for answers. I didn't get any until 15 years later.

One day in August 1984 I was contacted at work about a letter at the police station that needed to be picked up. It baffled me. I couldn't imagine what it was about. It was from someone named Doug Conn, my son's comrade.

That evening I phoned Doug in Boston. Doug thought it was odd that no one contacted him when he wrote the letter. He said that he had sent the letter in *February* of that year to the Chief of Police in Richmond, asking them for assistance in locating the family of Cary Miller. For reasons unknown to all of us, Doug's letter sat at the police station for six months!

After 15 years, I finally had answers. Doug's information contradicted the telegram stating Cary was killed instantly. Doug explained that Cary had fragmentation wounds in his chest, but was conscious for about 15 minutes. Doug explained that Cary *was aware* that Peter had been hurt, and had insisted that Doug go check on Peter. Doug left Cary for the moment to check on Peter's badly wounded leg. Cary had died by the time Doug could get back to him.

Cary and his comrades were in a unit called the Tomahawks. They're an active group that holds reunions in different cities. When the members came to Indiana for a reunion, they invited us to join them. We greeted them at the airport. We've been fortunate to attend their events throughout the years. The more we attend Tomahawk functions, the more we learn something about my son. One member related a time they were under fire and their ammunition was nearby in a large truck. If the truck had blown up, the entire group would have been trapped. Realizing the danger to his group, my son drove it out of the area before the enemy could locate it. They were a great support and we found answers about my son that no one else could provide.

My family and Linda are so grateful to the men of the Tomahawk unit. They eventually replaced the empty spot in our life that Cary's friends once filled. I realized it years later when my daughter held an anniversary party to honor Jess and me. She invited Cary's two high school buddies, Andy and Dennis. It was difficult for them to attend. Andy told me afterwards that he couldn't bear coming to our house and not seeing Cary. He said it had been hard for him to return–he just couldn't do it anymore. I understood perfectly and respect his feelings.

Unless you go through such an incredible loss, you have no idea what it is like. There is still a part inside that can never be replaced. Fortunately, I had a lot of support from my church and my family. I'm grateful that Kathy and her family are nearby and, of course, I still see Cary's fiancée, Linda. She is part of the family.

****

I felt as if I were right there with Marge and Linda as they searched for answers about Cary. When I asked Marge what she would say to Cary if he were here now, she related one last memory:

Cary wasn't one to stay out all night. He always came in, even if he worked late or was out with his buddies. He used to tease me saying, "I can go around that squeaky board in the floor and you don't know when I come in."

"I don't care what you think," I told him. "Every time you step through that door I am awake."

He was shocked. "You are?" My son didn't know it, but it wasn't the creaky board that woke me up when he came in. I used to hear him turning the key in the door. That is how I knew he was home. He never figured that out. If I could say something to Cary now, I would tell him, "I still wait for you and I listen for the key to turn in the door at night."

****

Marge's hospitality to me will never be forgotten. She is a lady of great strength and her family depended on her at the time of her son's death. Her daughter, Kathy, said that she never would've been able to get through her brother's death if it hadn't been for Marge.

Sadly, the little home that Jess and Cary built had to be razed. An interstate highway was constructed behind their house, forcing Marge to relocate. She doesn't hold any bitterness. Despite the loss of Cary to war and her husband, Jess, to Alzheimer disease, Marge maintains a cheerful, upbeat attitude as she cares for her family and her great-grandchildren.

Marjorie Miller

Private First Class Jack Wayne Miller, U.S. Army

Fountain City, Indiana

C Company, 22nd Infantry, 25th Division

Tay Ninh Province, Vietnam

KIA: January 2, 1968

Age: 20

"When I explained to him that we weren't Catholic,
his response was, 'It doesn't matter to a chaplain what
religion a man is when he is on a battlefield.'"

- Edith Miller

It was another scorching day in Indiana. I was driving toward Fountain City, impressed by the fact that here I was, a stranger, passing through vast open farmlands, searching to learn more about the experience of gold star mothers. I considered myself fortunate that two families from different towns would warmly welcome me into their homes, sharing stories about their sons from 35 years ago.

I pulled up to an older, neatly painted, two-story country home with an inviting front porch that overlooked a quiet, tree-lined street in town. Not a leaf stirred that morning in late June. An occasional car drove by, breaking the silence. I felt transported back to a more tranquil time in the life of small town America.

Edith and James Miller greeted me warmly at the door like a long lost relative. I felt as if I had stepped in to a July issue of "Better Homes and Gardens" magazine. Red, white, and blue burst forth as I gazed at the patriotic décor. Edith smiled proudly as I admired the flags, dolls, and decorations. The breathtaking room always looks like this—not just for the upcoming Fourth of July holiday. She said she loves her country. We continued to a cozy, country kitchen that overlooked a small garden in the backyard. As we sipped iced drinks at the kitchen table, I sensed a shyness in James as he sat next to his wife. Gray-haired, thinly built, and a bit nervous, he deferred to Edith as she spoke of their son. She gently touched his arm from time to time, almost as if she were reassuring him as she told her story. Edith began her story.

****

Jack Wayne Miller was our firstborn. He arrived on the birthday of our country, the fourth of July. My husband James and I couldn't have been prouder. A year after Jack, we had Carolyn. She entered the Army after graduating from high school and made a career in the military. We have two younger sons, Larry, and our baby, Jeff.

We struggled to make ends meet by working different shifts. From the time Jack was a baby, I worked nights at a nearby record company. It was a comfort knowing James was with him while I worked. I returned from work one evening and James related the following story.

Jack was a toddler and had just learned to walk. He was upset about something and began to fuss. James thought he was thirsty and gave him a bottle. James, exhausted from the day's work, sat down on the couch and started to doze off. Suddenly he felt a hard crack right between the eyes. It caught him with such force, the poor man thought his toes and nose had met instantly! When he opened his eyes, there in his lap was the baby bottle and Jack glaring at him!

James worked on a large hog farm when the kids were little. Jack accompanied him to work one Saturday afternoon to check on the 30 or 40 sows in the furring houses (birthing places). The sows were lying quietly in their pens with their piglets. As James walked down the rows to check on the sows, Jack stayed behind. James heard an occasional squeal coming from one of the babies. He turned back and called to Jack, asking what was going on. "Nothing," was Jack's reply. After a few more protesting squeals, James returned to where he last saw Jack. He noticed a hose was left out and it was giving off a fine mist. He watched Jack pick up the hose and run it over the piglets' legs. They disliked the feeling of cold water running down onto their feet so the little ones ran around, squealing and kicking their wet, hind legs straight up in the air!

James called out, "Jack, don't do that!" But Jack just laughed, finding it most amusing.

As he grew a bit older, my son helped James get the kids ready for bed. I remember hearing about the pranks they pulled while I was at work. Together, they used to give Jeff, the baby, his bath. He was perhaps, two or three years old at the time. After lifting him out of the bathtub and drying him off, Jack used to tell his little brother, "Close your eyes, Jeff, we have to get your night clothes over your head." Then Jack would slip my underwear or occasionally a half-slip over the baby's head. When the poor kid opened his eyes and looked in the mirror, he was dressed up like a woman. Poor Jeff would sit there bawling, while Jack and his dad laughed.

Truthfully, Jack was the best child a parent could have. I remember him building model cars and being an avid reader, especially mysteries. He was a well-rounded kid who loved school and did well. He wrote for the high school newspaper and excelled in art and choir.

My son graduated in 1965 from Fountain City High School, but we lacked funds for college. By then my husband was working for the Wayne County Highway Department, so Jack began working there with him. They often worked together, driving trucks and plowing the highways in winter. After working for a year at the highway department, my son had saved enough money to apply to Ball State University. He intended to study business administration and was preparing to leave for school when he got the call to serve his country. He didn't try to get out of it or get a deferment. I asked him what he was going to do. "I'll go and serve. I can go to college when I get back," he said.

Jack went to Fort Knox, Kentucky, for basic training, in the fall of 1966 and received combat training at Fort Polk, Louisiana. He landed in Vietnam April 1, 1967. He was stationed in Dau Ting, about 70 miles from Saigon, close to the Cambodian border. In the nine months that he was there, he never complained or said a thing about Vietnam. Only once did he ask me to go into the Dayton PX to pick up socks and shorts for him. Underclothes rotted right off of them in the hot jungles and couldn't be replaced fast enough. He said very little because he knew James and I worried a great deal.

****

As I listened to their story, the room was filling with a tension that I couldn't quite comprehend. James stood up and abruptly left the room, Edith explained in a low voice that James always had a haunting dream about Jack, but was unable to talk about it to others. She quietly continued:

Shortly before our son's last battle, James dreamed that he was in Vietnam with him. They were under attack and James was in a vulnerable, open spot. In the middle of the chaos and gunfire, Jack kept calling to his dad, urging him to come behind the big rock for protection, but James couldn't reach Jack. To this day, the nightmare still recurs.

The North Vietnamese and Vietcong agreed to a truce with the Americans for Christmas and New Year of 1967. They agreed not to attack American bases, yet they regrouped and planned their next attack when the truce ended. They came down Cambodian trails and infiltrated South Vietnam during that time.

One winter morning after Christmas vacation, our kids were getting ready for school. Jeff was in third grade. He was waiting for a classmate to come by and pick him up for school when the doorbell rang. He went to answer it, thinking it was his little friend, but it was the military. They informed us Jack had been killed on January 2, 1968. I was in shock and recall little of the funeral or days that followed. When they shipped his body home, I remember wanting to view our son one last time. The government gave strict orders that no one, including immediate family, could view him. It brought us no consolation or closure. James and I were so distraught. We wondered if perhaps there might have been a case of mistaken identity, but we learned there are five means of positively identifying a body. Jack had been identified by all of them. Our daughter, Carolyn, was serving in the Army at the time. She tried to find out the details leading up to his death, but the government would not release any information to her.

We waited for someone to contact us and explain what happened. The days turned into months and the months became years. The war in Southeast Asia had ended, but it never ended for us. Two decades had passed. James and I were grandparents. I held on to hope that someone would contact us about the night of January 2, 1968.

I met another Gold Star Mother, Marge Miller, whose son Cary Miller had died in Vietnam. We became friends and compared notes about our sons' deaths. We discovered that neither of us knew what happened to our sons. In 1985, 14 years after Cary's death, Marge told me that she had finally found out details about her son through the men he served with in his group. No one from my son's group contacted me. It was clear that I would have to do the searching if I was going have answers.

In 1991 I sat down and began writing letters to different veterans' organizations, asking if anyone knew my son while in Vietnam. I received a few replies from those who knew of the battle, yet no one knew him personally. Twenty-eight years had now passed; I still had no answers.

One day in 1995, I ran into Danny Alexander, an old friend of Jack's from high school. We had lost touch with him after Jack graduated. Danny and my son had served in the 22nd Infantry of the 25th Division. When I explained that I was trying to obtain a list of men who served with Jack, Danny inquired and provided me with the names. I began my search again. I contacted 14 men, asking each if he had known Jack and if he could tell me what had happened to my son on January 2. My prayers were answered. Thirteen men responded. Some wrote, while others called. Everybody contributed something, but one person in particular will remain close to my heart. Finally, I had heard from someone who had been with my son in his last hours.

Coy Thomas, a gentleman from Illinois, called us. He said for 28 years he had been trying to muster the courage to stop in and talk with us, but he always turned around and headed back home. Coy felt that Jack should've survived, that it should've been Coy who was gone. They had changed shifts that night.

Coy said Jack was on duty out on a listening post the night of the attack. Jack had to sit quietly and listen for anyone approaching in the dark. He heard the enemy coming and called back to the camp to warn them. The North Vietnamese greatly outnumbered the Americans. They overran the camp.

Coy further explained that another young boy with Jack became hysterical as the North Vietnamese invasion began. Jack went over to reassure the boy and sent him back to camp. Once the boy got back into the perimeter, they asked him where Jack was. He told them that Jack was coming, but our son never returned. When the fighting ended, they went out to the listening post to see what had happened. They found Jack. Apparently, he and an enemy soldier had killed each other in hand-to-hand combat.

We received more information from Chaplain Jim Tobin who wrote and shared his memories. He turned out be one of the most comforting people that I have ever known. When I asked Chaplain Tobin if he knew Jack personally, he said he did not. Unfortunately there were so many soldiers; the chaplains don't get to know each one individually. Chaplain Jim was Catholic and administered Last Rites to his fallen comrades. I explained that we weren't Catholic. "It doesn't matter to a chaplain what religion a man is when he is on a battlefield," he said.

I was so grateful. I told him it didn't matter to me whatsoever. I was glad that he had been there for my son. After the war was over, Chaplain Tobin spent a year working in Washington, D.C. where the Vietnam Memorial was built. He often went over to The Wall and spent many hours in front of it, finding names of those to whom he administered Last Rites. I will always remember how he comforted James and me with these words, "I didn't know Jack personally the night of the battle in Vietnam, but I've gone to The Wall many times. It was there that I did meet him personally." I will always be indebted to the men from our son's unit who shared their memories with us.

If there is something I want the rest of the country to know about my son, it's that he was proud to go and serve. If I could tell him something now, I would say, "Jack, we love you and miss you so much in our home. Some days it seems like just yesterday that it happened and other days, it seems like a million years have gone by."

****

I reflected on my visit to Indiana as I began my eight-hour drive home to Buffalo. I was touched by the Millers' pride in their son. This humble, hard-working couple had struggled all their lives and welcomed me into their home. I later understood why their house was so special to them. When Jack's parents received his insurance benefit, they used it as a down payment toward the purchase of this home—the first one they ever owned.

James and Edith Miller with the author

*

WILSON B KEE

Specialist 4
Wilson Begay Kee,
U.S. Army

Cottonwood, Arizona

2nd Platoon, A Company, 21st Infantry Regiment,
11th Infantry Brigade

Quang Ngai Province, Vietnam

KIA: June 17, 1970

Age: 22

"Enough is enough! Didn't we learn from Vietnam?
War is still going on today."

- Sadie Kee

Thomas Gorman at the Department of Navajo Veteran Affairs in Arizona, introduced me to two Navajo mothers who had lost sons in Vietnam, one from Leupp, Arizona and the other from Cottonwood. Sadie B. Kee of Cottonwood was a petite, 90-pound lady with graying hair neatly pulled back in a pony tail. Tom explained Navajo customs and beliefs and he translated Sadie's story. Sadie's family is a patriotic one. Not only did her son, Wilson, serve as an infantryman in Vietnam, her son, Harrison, served there as a Navy SEAL. One grandson, Vernan, served in Afghanistan. I drove to Cottonwood on a hot August day. Waves of heat shimmered off the parched earth. Houses in this bare, open country were two miles apart. When I found Sadie's house, I proceeded up the mile-long driveway and ended at a little, white concrete block ranch. I entered a simple and cheerful kitchen with clean cut tile floors. In Sadie's living room, pictures of her children and grandchildren covered the walls and shelves. Centered among the photos was one of Wilson. As I listened to Sadie's story, I was informed that there is no term for "hero" in the Navajo language. The best translation is the term, "a respected person."

****

My son Wilson was the oldest of 13 children. As a young boy he was most responsible. From an early age he took the lead and went out in the fields, planting corn and various crops. It was a large area to be responsible for, yet those were his happiest times. He loved the outdoors more than anything. One of my fondest memories was watching Wilson learn from his dad. My husband had a great influence on our son. He was a wise man, and instructed him well. Though he worked on the railroad and was absent frequently, he taught Wilson a great deal. Our son was also wise. He in turn, taught his eight brothers and four sisters what he had learned, setting a good example as a hard worker.

Wilson was quiet, almost shy, around people he didn't know well. Around his friends or other boys, he was much more comfortable. When he was with his siblings, he played pranks and he was the biggest tease.

One particular memory remains of when he was a teenager. He went out one day to visit someone and took Louise, his younger sister, with him. While they were out, he suddenly got up and told Louise it was time for them to leave and that she had to drive the truck home. She was only twelve years old at the time! She told him she didn't know the first thing about driving a truck. He gave her quick instructions. She came in very scared, but said she was careful. She drove a standard shift from that day on.

My son had two pastimes. One was baseball. As a teenager, he patiently played ball with brothers and sisters, but he preferred to play baseball with his friends. His other interest stands out vividly. Wilson was an excellent bronco rider and loved taming horses. We always had wild mustangs on our property, up on a ridge behind our house. He broke the horses in. To watch a youth get tossed around as he hung on to a wild horse was hilarious, but Wilson was very good with animals and seemed to understand their nature. He rode and trained with his cousin, Danny. Wilson's younger brother, Thomas Jr., also went along with the two boys, so the three of them spent time together, riding and taming the horses. Those were the best times for my son and also the best memories I have of him as he grew up.

There was one particular red horse, a roan that Wilson was especially successful with, and it became his favorite among those that we had. He never named it, but after some time we always knew what horse he had taken out. If he was gone, so was the roan. Wilson and his favorite companion stayed around the open areas of our house, yet it was an important part in his daily routine, as he used the roan to check on the animals and crops. My mother lived about 25 miles away, in Salina Springs, so he often rode his horse to her house to pay a visit.

For Wilson, nothing compared to nature. He used to go up into the mountains and spend the day there with his cousins, cooking outdoors. It was a great adventure for all of them. One winter we had a great deal of snow, and the kids had the idea of hauling firewood from the mountains by creating a sled. They got a hood from an old car, turned it upside down and hitched it up to a horse. They piled wood on it and brought it in. It was work, but Wilson and his brothers found it fun.

Like most children on the reservation, he attended the Bureau of Indian Affairs School in Chinle. He later transferred to a public school but didn't graduate. From there, he took a job on the railroad and worked with his father in another area.

One day, while he was home, he informed us that he had signed up to serve his country. I was unprepared for this. He hadn't consulted my husband or me about his decision. We didn't know he was even thinking of serving his country. Within a few days, he left for Albuquerque where he was inducted into the Army. We didn't hear from him for the longest time. He completed his basic training in California and then wrote home explaining how he was with a group that did a lot of mock combat training in the woods and mountains of California.

There was only one time that my son was granted a leave. He returned home for 12 days in November during Thanksgiving. Wilson spent a lot of time with his family, especially with my son, Thomas. He was happy just to be home, and I was thrilled just to see him again. Thanksgiving held such special memories. Before I knew it, his furlough was over. He flew out of Albuquerque and from there to Vietnam. That was the last time I saw him.

My husband didn't serve in the military, but Wilson was extremely patriotic and felt deeply about serving in Vietnam. He always assured us that he was going to be okay and that he would return safely. He rarely wrote home. He was able to phone often, though. We didn't have a phone of our own, so he would call my sister, his Aunt Tullie, who lived in Chinle. She would come over and tell us when he called.

I have very few facts about my son's death. He was in Quang Ngai Province when he died. When two military personnel arrived to notify us of the horrible news my husband was home with me and tried to console me. The only knowledge we have about his death is that he died from some kind of land mine explosive and was killed instantly. His casket had to remain closed at his funeral.

At the time of my son's death, I didn't know about the American Gold Star Mothers organization. It was many years later that I learned of it, so I never became a member. There were four other families in Chinle who lost sons in Vietnam, but I was not in contact with them. I remained by myself and tended closely to my 12 children, keeping a very quiet life. They, along with my husband, were my greatest support. I have several sisters, but they lived far from here at the time of Wilson's death. With no phone, I had little contact with them. Fortunately I have an older brother nearby who was a great support.

I did not go out in public much, so I never knew how the community felt or responded. There was no ceremony or tribute in my son's honor at the time of his death, such as a dedication or a memorial. It was not until many years later that I saw an acknowledgement of my son's sacrifice.

When I was told that my son had been killed in action, I didn't believe it. I still feel that way sometimes. Once in a while I think that he's out there somewhere. I like to believe he might return—that there's hope. When I see a serviceman or someone in a military uniform, I feel that I'm going to see Wilson again soon. There is a military cemetery located in Fort Defiance, a small town outside of Window Rock, Arizona, and my son is buried there.

I saw the Traveling Wall when it came to Window Rock. It was overwhelming and so emotional. I was broken-hearted. I had never been to The Wall in Washington, D.C.

****

After I left Sadie's home, it was a few months before I completed her story. I mailed it to Tom Gorman who translated it into Navajo for Sadie to approve. Sadie's daughter contacted me and told me that my visit made an impression on Tom Gorman and the veterans in her town, who were touched by her story. Subsequently, Sadie received a surprise, as we will go on to hear.

****

Then I received a surprise. The Veterans Association from Chinle invited me to accompany them on Veterans Day weekend, in order to observe the ceremony that took place in Washington, D.C. On Veterans Day, 2007, the Vietnam Veterans were celebrating the twenty-fifth anniversary of the dedication of The Wall. My daughter, Linda, went with me and felt so privileged to be invited. My son Harrison met us there. It was my first time on an airplane and the first I have ever traveled so far from home.

On Friday, they took me to the eastern shore and I saw the Atlantic Ocean. On Saturday, a parade was dedicated to veterans of all nationalities, including those from the Navajo Nation. They wanted me to be in the parade with them as a gold star mother, but I felt more comfortable as a spectator. They were most understanding of my feelings. On Sunday they took me to The Wall, and there I actually saw Wilson's name engraved. I experienced a sense of some relief. It lifted many burdens. The fact that my son is gone is now a reality that we will all have to live with.

Seeing the WWII and Vietnam memorials, along with the women veterans and other gold star mothers was very emotional for me as well as my family. I was so joyful that I was able to witness for myself what I had only seen on television or as a picture in a magazine. It was most important to me. I have many pictures from that unforgettable trip.

****

As the interview came to a close, I asked Sadie what she'd like to say to the country about her son. Her dark eyes blazed and riveting words came forth:

If I could tell the country and those in Washington something about my son I'd say to the president, the lawmakers and people responsible for allowing young men to still go to war, "Enough is enough! Didn't we learn from Vietnam? War is still going on today. Why don't you understand that? Our kids are still fighting for us now! We need to value our kids!"

****

Nearly four decades later, after her trip to Washington, D.C., Sadie had finally received support. She is now connected to other mothers who lost sons in the Vietnam War and she now feels that our nation does indeed recognize her son Wilson as "a respected person."

Sadie Kee

Specialist 4
Bennie Leo Huskon,
U.S. Army

Leupp, Arizona

163rd Supply Company, 506th Field Depot

Gia Dinh Province, Vietnam

KIA: June 7, 1968

Age: 21

"He died for a person who will die of old age. He died
for a baby who will be born today."

- Emma Jean Willie

The day after I met with Sadie B. Kee in Chinle, I again drove across the desert of the Navajo Nation to meet with American Gold Star Mother Emma Jean Willie, mother of Bennie Huskon. The relentless August sun beat down on a cluster of white stucco ranches situated on the outskirts of town. Nothing stirred as the heat waves reflected off the homes, cacti and desert floor. Emma Jean's simple, but neat, one-floor home seemed to bake beneath the desert heat. Her daughter, Delores Lee, greeted me at the door. She had attended college and was fluent in English. She would translate for her mother who spoke only Navajo. One of Emma's sons and his wife proudly sat next to her. As we sat around the table, I sensed the family's closeness. Pictures of her son, Bennie Huskon, were placed on the table, showing me a young boy, a teenager and later, a serviceman. Emma Jean spoke about her son.

****

My son Bennie was my first child and I was very proud when he arrived on May 21, 1947. We were now a family of three, but only for a brief time. When he was one month old, my husband passed away. In his absence I had many lonely moments. Family members stepped in a great deal to help Bennie and me, so this provided the security we both needed. My family adored him and I recall how his uncles lovingly carried him around.

He was a quiet boy, not very talkative, but occasionally he would comment on something. As a young child, my son only spoke Navajo; however, his Aunt Marie spoke English. One of my fondest moments was when he was three years old. One day his Aunt Marie took him to the Leupp Trading Post and Bennie silently watched as his aunt carried on a transaction in English with the trader's wife, Mrs. McGee. The conversation in English baffled him. After his aunt purchased a can of coffee, Bennie followed her out. When he arrived home, his uncle asked him, "Bennie, what was the trip to the store like?"

Bennie's interpretation of the afternoon was, "Aunt Marie *mumbled* something to the lady and then got a can of coffee."

As he grew up, he was such an obedient boy. He never talked back or said anything harsh to me. When he was seven, he started school in Old Leupp. His favorite teacher, Mr. Lloyd Lewis, was a talented man who taught several grades at once in a one-room schoolhouse. Bennie's favorite sport while at school was basketball.

He took an interest in two other activities. He loved music; a big part of his life was playing the guitar. As he practiced with his friends, I still remember him singing, "I Got a Tiger by the Tail" by Buck Owens and "North to Alaska" by Johnny Horton. Those songs are rooted in my memory.

Bennie's second love was the outdoors. A great deal of his life was spent outside with our family. It was his favorite activity and he found so many things to do. He farmed, planted corn or squash, and herded sheep. He and his little brothers used to walk across the Little Colorado River, proceed several miles toward Canyon Diablo and hunt rabbits. They then brought them home to cook for dinner. He also enjoyed hunting deer and elk with his uncles and grandfather. They camped out for days as they hunted, skinned and cleaned the animals.

My love for horses and riding must have rubbed off on my son. He enjoyed horses also, so one year when my mare had a foal, I presented it to him for his birthday. He loved the gentle brown horse with white patches and named it Wheaty. He trained the horse and eventually rode him. They were inseparable. Bennie loved riding him throughout the Leupp area with his two friends, Norman Kaye and Jim Store.

I eventually remarried after the death of Bennie's father. As my family grew, Bennie came to have younger brothers and sisters who considered him very exciting and looked up to him. They often asked for a ride on Wheaty, making Bennie feel obliged, but sometimes they paid the price. One time his younger sister Emily pestered him too much so he took her on a ride—a wild ride. She remembers falling off the horse in the process.

Emily had humorous moments with Bennie and found ways to even the score. I recall the day a dog was on our front porch. Bennie was expecting one of his friends to come by the house at that moment. Emily heard a sound that appeared to be a knock at the front door, so she opened it. There stood the dog, his tail rapidly wagging back and forth against the door. Emily closed the door and went over to Bennie's room.

"Your friend is here," she informed him. Bennie came out of his room and opened the door. There was the dog with its wagging tail.

As he got older, Bennie's interest turned to vehicles and he acquired a motorcycle. He enjoyed driving it around Leupp. His younger siblings' interest also turned from Wheaty to the motorcycle, and once again, they pestered him for rides.

My son John was still quite young, perhaps under 10, when he got the ride of his life one day. John and his friends were skinny-dipping down at a local swimming hole. At the end of the day, he asked Bennie for a ride back. Bennie couldn't refuse the chance to honor his request, so as they left the swimming hole, Bennie placed his little brother on the motorcycle and headed home. John never forgot that ride. As they came back home, Bennie drove through the town of Leupp with his little brother on the seat, stark naked!

During holidays like Christmas and Thanksgiving, my son spent a great deal of time with his aunt, my oldest sister. He learned to cook while helping her prepare for the large family gatherings that she hosted. He enjoyed it immensely and made very good stews and bean dishes. He used to ask his younger sister, Delores, to make a certain fried bread that accompanied his bean dishes. He even baked at times and I remember him preparing a favorite dessert, lemon meringue pie. He also made cakes with delicious homemade frostings. He really was a generous kid, who used his cooking skills for our family. His sister Emily remembers Bennie giving her a party for her fourteenth birthday—and he made the cake for her.

My son finished elementary school in Leupp, and later attended high school in Flagstaff, Arizona. It was a boarding school, about an hour west of our home and it was there that he met his girlfriend, Phyllis. He received a good education, but the distance didn't allow him the opportunity to come home often. He only returned home for one weekend each month. He graduated from high school in 1967. In the summer, shortly after his graduation, he enlisted in the Army.

Bennie's classmates in Flagstaff, Leroy Nelson and Jackie Williams, were enlisting at the same time. Norman Kaye, his best friend from childhood, had also enlisted. Bennie completed basic training at Fort Bliss, Texas and then continued on to Fort Lee, Virginia for some time. He did well there and in February 1968, he wrote home saying he had been promoted to Specialist 4th Class.

He came home for a two-week furlough in March 1968. When his leave was up on March 28, we saw him off from the Flagstaff bus station at one o'clock in the afternoon. As he left, I remember him waving to us. We stood there crying. The ride home was quiet. Each one of us was lost in our own thoughts of my son. His bus journey from Flagstaff continued on to Phoenix, Los Angeles and then Oakland, California, where he spent the night.

Two days later, on March 30, 1968, Bennie left for Vietnam. I remember the time frame of his trip. It took him five hours to get to Hawaii and from there, 12 to the Philippine Islands and then two to Vietnam. We quickly learned that Vietnam's jungles and highlands were not the only dangerous areas. Bennie wrote his sister, Delores, on April 8th, stating that on the evening he arrived in Bien Hoa, they instantly came under a mortar attack. Though he didn't write often, his letter spoke volumes when he commented about the unexpected attack, saying, "We only had a few casualties."

The odds are unlikely that two boys from a small town like Leupp would meet in the same place halfway around the world, but at the base in Bien Hoa, my son met a former classmate, David Little. They attended school together here in Leupp. It was a surprise for my son because he hadn't seen David in years.

Bennie continued on to Saigon where he was later stationed. It was a striking contrast from the open, rural area of Leupp where he grew up and explored for days on end. He was in awe of the Saigon traffic. He wrote home and commented humorously, saying:

> The city of Saigon is interesting. The traffic here is like a triple Flagstaff pow-wow all the time!

My son was in administration, as an office accountant with the 163rd Supply Company, a branch of the 506th Field Depot. He had the opportunity to work with the Vietnamese. The entire time he was at the base in Saigon, a Vietnamese girl served as his administrative assistant. While he was in Vietnam he did not receive a paycheck as we know it. He was paid the equivalent of 270 dollars per month in something called scrip. It was a certificate of a right to exchange for items such as money or goods at the PX.

On the surface, his job appeared safe but my son could sense the dangers. He didn't write home often, and when he did, I remember him saying that he didn't know if he'd make it back. The large depots were susceptible to bombing and attacks, just like any rural outpost. In one letter he said:

I think I'm all right now, but it still isn't that safe because we get attacked every once in a while, especially here at the air base.

Bennie wanted to serve in Vietnam, and when he volunteered to go, he knew there was a strong possibility he'd be sent there. He felt strongly about the Vietnam War. My second husband, George Boyd Willie, Bennie's stepfather, served in the Pacific as a Navajo Code Talker during World War II. His job was considered classified, and he was not allowed to discuss the nature of his work for about 25 years, until the late 1960s. With that in mind, I don't think he influenced Bennie's military decision. Bennie enlisted on his own. My husband remained silent and kept his opinions to himself when Bennie decided to volunteer.

My son was in Saigon a little more than two months when the base was hit by a mortar attack in June. He and another young man were fatally injured. I also heard that a third young man, one of Bennie's classmates from high school in Flagstaff, was killed that same day.

My family and I were at church on the day we were notified of my son's death. We were attending a funeral for a friend. As the funeral ended and we were leaving the church, a military vehicle pulled up. Someone asked the military personnel why they were there. It was then that they notified me that my son had been killed on the previous Friday. How ironic. At the moment I was leaving a funeral, I was told the news.

I always hoped someone would contact me with further knowledge about my son's death. One comrade, George Morris, who had served with Bennie in Fort Lee, Virginia, later contacted our family; however, he hadn't served with Bennie in Vietnam. Other than that, I have never been contacted by any of his comrades from Vietnam, so I have never learned the circumstances or details of his death.

My son is buried in the Leupp Cemetery. The only compensation we received from the Army was a ten thousand dollar life insurance policy. That was nothing compared to the loss of my son.

Each family member grieved the loss differently. My daughter, Delores, received the last letter that he wrote, and it arrived after his death. The entire community was affected by his death. Family, friends, relatives and even our church came forward to offer support. I was not aware of any other support group, such as the American Gold Star Mothers. I didn't know of any grief counseling at the time for mothers like me who lost sons in war. I suffered a great deal from the loss of my eldest son. It was many years later when I finally received counseling, but most of all, it was my God who helped me through this difficult period. I am a person of great faith. My son's death only strengthened my faith. It did not weaken it. My hope is to one day rejoice with him in heaven.

He was in Vietnam just over a month, when he sent me a big Bible. It arrived just before his twenty first birthday, on May 21. It was just a few weeks later that he was killed. I not only have this precious Bible, I also have his Bible that was returned with his belongings from Vietnam. In it are certain pages with folded corners and underlined passages.

I am familiar with the loss of life for our country. I grew up in a family that has served this country with pride. Not only was my husband a Navajo Code Talker, but my uncle, Charles Kelly, served in World War II and the Korean War. My older brother, Norman Kelly, was killed in World War II. He is buried at the National Cemetery in Santa Fe, New Mexico. My three older brothers, Bert Kelly, Robert Kelly and Billy Schultz also served in the military. My son Justin served in the Marines, and my grandson, Randall Smallcanyon, is presently serving in the Marines. My daughter, Emily, wanted to enlist in the service, but I talked her out of it.

The American Legion Post, named after a World War II veteran, was later renamed to include Bennie's name. I have since become an Auxiliary Member of the Curtis-Huskon Post, American Legion Post 112. The Tuba City Vietnam Veterans presented me with a shawl since I am a gold star mother, and I treasure it. When I walk in parades or attend pow-wow events, I wear it in honor of my son.

I have been to the Vietnam Memorial Wall in Washington three times. My first visit was in May of 1988. My daughter Delores took us on the trip to help us deal with our grief. Our last visit, in August of 2007, was a memorable experience. I was able to see his name as I walked along. I have also seen the Traveling Wall three times when it came to the area.

Eventually I joined and I have remained active in the AGSM organization to provide support to Navajo mothers who have lost sons or daughters in Iraq or Afghanistan. I have also been an advocate for veterans. They need to receive better benefits, such as healthcare and housing. It is vital that we show respect to our veterans for their service to this country.

****

As the interview came to a close, I asked Delores what her mother would like our country to know about Bennie. Emma Jean lowered her eyes, and in a soft, low voice, she spoke in Navajo for several minutes. Everyone's eyes were on her. A moment of panic fluttered in my stomach as everyone sat so still and Delores stopped translating. I had no idea what was being said or what Delores would later tell me. When Emma Jean finished, Delores emphasized how her mother wanted to thank me for coming so far to listen to her story about her son, Bennie. Emma Jean wanted us to know this about her son:

****

My son gave his life for his country like so many others who lost their lives in all the wars. He didn't hesitate to defend his country. I've been told by leaders and by my people that my son did not die in vain. I feel that my son defended our freedom and our country. He died for a person who will die of old age. He died for a baby who will be born today.

If I could tell my son something, I would tell him I remember him and I love him. I would tell him he is in a better place, a happier place. I would tell him I talk to him when I look at his picture.

****

This was a particularly moving interview as was my whole trip to the Southwest. As I drove away through the stark but tranquil landscape, I felt honored to know so many of the fine people who lived there.

George B. and Emma Jean Willie

Private First Class Robert Benjamin Luther, U.S. Army

Grand Island, New York

D Company, 1st Battalion, 11th Infantry Regiment,
5th Infantry Division

Base Fuller

Quang Tri Province, Vietnam

KIA: May 10, 1970

Age: 21

"I can only conclude that there's no rhyme or reason
for what happens in situations like these when parents
lose a son or daughter."

- Shirley Luther

Robert Luther grew up in a neat, Cape Cod-style house on Grand Island, New York. Grand Island is located on the Niagara River, between the U.S. and Canada. Gold Star Mother Shirley Luther still tends the home where her children grew up. On the day I visited her, she proudly showed me around her house. We sat down at a table in the family room that overlooked a park-like back yard. She shared photos of her son, talking quietly about the letters he sent home from Vietnam.

****

During the seven months that he was in Vietnam, I eagerly waited for letters from my son, Robert. He didn't write often nor did he say much, but one thing he did say in his letters was:

> I know why we're over here. I just wish it were for a different reason.

I always remembered that. He never elaborated on it, but he seemed sad at the time that he wrote it. He was a real sensitive kid and I think he saw things in Vietnam that they weren't free to talk about. They were there for the war part, of course, but I'm sure he saw things going on and that was why he wished that it was for a different reason, such as helping the impoverished people rather than bringing such war and destruction to the Vietnamese and their country. My husband never commented on Bob's statement. To this day I still wonder exactly what my son meant.

I think back on what my son could have been and what he might have accomplished. Even after all these years, I still picture him contributing to a community, wherever he would've resided. I think he would've been a good family man and a good, solid citizen. I couldn't see him ever demonstrating or ever being on drugs and drinking. It wasn't his nature. He had good values. He knew what he stood for and how he felt about his country.

We discussed numerous topics. Vietnam was among them. Before entering the service, we discussed the draft dodging issue. He could've gone to Canada. It's a stone's throw from our house—less than a mile across the Niagara River. But Bob didn't think that way. "No, if I have to go to Vietnam, then I'll go," he said. Sometimes I ask myself why I didn't encourage him to go to Canada.

But on the other hand, I'm still so proud of him. I remember when there was talk about amnesty for those who refused to go to Vietnam and instead went to Canada. I wrote a letter to Senator Ted Kennedy stating I was so upset that our government wanted to allow the draft dodgers to return and be forgiven with no penalty at all. Yet all my thoughts won't change anything, no matter what.

Our photo albums and scrapbooks remind me of all the activities he participated in. Bob was our only son. His older sister, Nancy, and two younger sisters, Gail and Carol, adored him. As a young boy, he labored patiently for hours, making model cars and ships, but he enjoyed the outdoors most of all. The best vacations were family camping trips in a pop-up tent trailer. All outdoor activities appealed to him, like Boy Scouts, summer youth camps sponsored by Trinity United Methodist Church or fishing on the island shore with his sister, Nancy.

I recall a touching memory of my son as a small boy. Whenever I wore an apron he had a habit of sneaking up on me, and he'd gently untie it. I'd turn around and there he was, grinning as the apron hung loosely from my neck.

Bob played the trumpet in middle school and continued with the high school band, but most of all he loved sports. His dad coached him in Little League baseball, and he continued playing through high school. Grand Island is close to Niagara Falls, but high school students attended school on the mainland in Buffalo or the City of Tonawanda. Eventually the need arose for a high school on the Island. Bob's class was the first to graduate from the newly built Grand Island High School in June 1966.

What stands out most was Bob's love for football, his favorite sport. In his senior year he was a 5'10" 155-pound halfback for the 1965-1966 Grand Island Varsity Football team. He was incredibly disciplined when he worked out. He ate as much as he wanted, so mealtime was hassle-free and enjoyable.

After football, wrestling followed in the winter and required a different discipline. Then he fought to keep his weight down. I used to get so angry with him because he wouldn't eat. He'd get annoyed with me because I was always after him to eat! His wrestling coach kept Bob's best interest in mind. He wanted Bob to continue wrestling after graduation. I think he not only saw Bob's potential as an outstanding athlete, but he also hoped that it might be an incentive to keep him in college for four years rather than just two. That would've increased his chance for a deferment. Yet my son wanted no part of a four-year commitment to college. He was good in math and completed his associate's degree in engineering from Erie Community College in 1968. After that, he'd had enough of school and chose not to go on for a bachelor's degree. He worked for a year, applying his engineering skills at an architectural firm and at the Grand Island Engineering Department.

My son knew his notice to serve would come once he finished college, so he wasn't surprised when he was drafted a year later, in June 1969. His sister Nancy was about to be married at that time so he appealed the induction date, asking if he could postpone it a few days in order to be in her wedding. I was glad he appealed it. They granted him the postponement and he was able to celebrate her wedding on Saturday, June 21. By Monday, June 23, he left for the service. That was the last time my son saw his sister Nancy and her new airman husband Rick. They moved to an Air Force base in Charleston, South Carolina. Bob left for Fort Dix, New Jersey to begin basic training.

He completed his eight-week basic training and managed to get home a couple of times. He wasn't supposed to—but he did! His younger sisters, Carol and Gail, used to laugh and tease him when he came in the door because he looked so different with his head shaved. Two months later, in October, he was sent to Fort Lewis, Washington. We worried about his future, but he told us that his orders were to go to Germany. Then, the night before he was to be shipped out to Germany, he called me. "My orders have been changed and I'm going to Vietnam," he said. Unfortunately, my son wasn't granted a leave to return home before shipping out.

Bob was in the infantry but we knew very little about his work. Soldiers were not free to discuss their jobs, so when he wrote, it was often just a brief statement that he was fine or that he had received a package. Letters didn't arrive immediately back then like the e-mail and text messaging we have today. I'm amazed by the fact that parents can talk to their sons and daughters wherever they're stationed throughout the world, or send an e-mail that arrives in seconds. With cell phones and web cams, they can hear their kids' voices and even see them. They can learn so much more now about their kids' conditions and how they're doing while in combat. Who could even imagine back then, that this would be the way to communicate with your kids when they go off to war? Waiting was a big part of my life while Bob was in Vietnam. Either I waited weeks for a letter from him, or he waited weeks for letters and packages from me. I saved his hand written letters. They're something I can look back on—memories to touch, which technology doesn't offer.

Mothers Day is always a bad time for me. It's the anniversary of my son's death. Something unusual occurred on Mothers Day that particular year. Maybe it was just a coincidence—I can't say for sure. Unknown to me, Bob had asked his girlfriend Ruth to order flowers for me as a Mothers' Day gift. When they arrived, I placed the beautiful yellow bouquet of roses in the front room on the television, next to his picture. We were having dinner in the dining room that Sunday with the windows open. All of a sudden a gust of wind came in and blew my son's picture over. I turned around saw his picture face down. "Boy, I hope that doesn't mean anything," I said.

On Tuesday morning, two days after Mothers Day, I brought a newspaper article into work for the ladies in my office to read. I wanted to show them what a difficult time these boys were having in Southeast Asia. The article was dated Monday, May 11, Khe Go Bridge, Vietnam. It stated that fierce fighting had occurred. Americans based in Da Nang had gone up a mountain to a camp called Base Fuller. It had been under a 43-day siege. I knew Bob was stationed at Da Nang, but I didn't know at the time that he was on the mission with that particular group. The article went on to say that they met heavy enemy fire and were pursued by the enemy as they tried to come back down the mountain. As the American troops retreated, a helicopter passing overhead was hit by enemy ground fire. It came down and crashed among the Americans, killing all six Americans who were onboard as well as one soldier on the ground. On late Tuesday afternoon, Army officials came to the office where I worked. They told me about my son's death. He had been the soldier on the ground when the helicopter was hit by enemy fire.

My husband was devastated and the loss was so hard for my three daughters. Nancy and her husband lived out of town. Gail and Carol were still at home, so I had to keep them and Bob's fiancée, Ruth, buoyed up. Gail was 19 and working at the time. Bob had always been concerned about her health and had always been protective of both his sisters. Carol, our youngest, was only 15 and it was especially tough on her. She used to come home from school saying, "Everybody looks at me. Why don't they leave me alone?"

Truthfully, I think everyone felt so bad that they simply didn't know what to say. My husband was active in politics on Grand Island so everyone knew us. The community was most supportive and all the flags were flown at half staff. Our church congregation knew Bob through the youth fellowship program and was a great comfort at the time.

A plaque was later placed in the foyer of Grand Island High School in recognition of the servicemen from Grand Island who sacrificed their lives in Vietnam. The families of the servicemen were deeply touched by such a kind act. I want my daughters to always remember their brother and his sacrifice. When events like these come up, I try to give each of my daughters items related to their brother such as a set of pictures, or articles that I come across. Hopefully, each one will have things about him to remember.

It was hard for me to imagine Bob's living conditions and what he saw over there. Some of his personal belongings were returned, providing insight to his life in Southeast Asia. He took slides that were later returned. Yet, from what I figured out, I knew there had to be more slides so I sent a note to the company where they were developed, requesting that the remaining slides be sent to me. Eventually they arrived, presenting a better picture of his life. Judging from them, I would say that they certainly ate their share of C-Rations. It is a comfort to know Bob had received photos of his first niece, Kelly, born in March. But perhaps most important among Bob's personal belongings were names and addresses of some soldiers he had served with, both in the States and in Vietnam. I wanted to know more about my son, so I wrote to his comrades. I wanted to see what they knew, and I asked if they could tell me anything.

One young man wrote back and said he didn't even know that my son had been killed until he heard from me. They had been together in Fort Lewis, but later became separated in Vietnam. It must have been hard for these guys to become good friends in basic training and then be shipped off to a country where they were split up, never knowing what happened to each other.

Another friend, Mike Sperling, responded at length to my letters. I was grateful for what he told me about the brief time he served with my son. Bob had met him in basic training. Eventually, they were stationed together at Fort Lewis. Mike was from that area, and when he replied to my inquiry about Bob, he related a humorous incident about the two of them before they left for Vietnam.

"We got the idea that we would cheat and stay with our families for the weekend and come back to Fort Lewis on Sunday evening—what could they do to us? Send us to Nam? We were already going!" I was deeply touched by something else Mike wrote. "He did the right thing and died. I didn't and lived." I think he must have felt guilt that he survived and my son didn't. I imagine a lot of them feel that way.

Bob had met his fiancée, Ruth, through his younger sister Gail. She was a real nice girl and they went steady. They had planned on marrying after he got out of the service, so Bob's death left her heartbroken. We included Ruth in everything our family did. It was so tough on her. She was such a sweet girl, and I felt as if she were a fourth daughter. I tried to comfort her in all these dark moments. Ruth later married, but it wasn't until about five years after Bob's death. She had children and seems quite happy, which is the way it should be. She lives nearby in the city of Lockport and we still keep in touch to this day.

Grand Island has a beautiful area called Veterans Park that contains several baseball diamonds. One diamond was recently renamed in honor of Bob. Ruth attended the ceremony and that was the first I had seen her in a couple of years. The loss from 40 years ago still leaves me wondering what could have been, had he returned. Ruth would've been such a wonderful daughter-in-law. I feel certain that she and my son would still be together, because she's not the type to have broken up with him. He was like that, too. They shared similar family values. He was a very sound kid and looking at them I felt very comfortable that things would've been very good. Ruth was Roman Catholic but we were not. Bob attended church with her in the morning and then came home and attended Trinity United Methodist Church with me. That's the kind of kid that he was—so understanding and such a good person. I often wonder where they would be now if Bob had returned home—what they'd be doing and if they would've had children. It was tough for all of us. I think of her often, and have tried to accept the fact that it just was not meant to be—for her as well as for us.

I would never care to relive the 10 years following Bob's death. I couldn't wait until the 70s decade was over. We lost our son in May of 1970 and then my two daughters lost three babies during the 70s. My husband lost an election and stayed out of politics for a while. Later, he returned and served as town supervisor for 10 years. Special events came along like the birth of my grandchildren, but those ten years up to 1980 were either a very high or very low time. Fortunately, my husband had a huge support base of friends in politics along with members from the Grand Island Fire Company. They helped him get through our son's death during those years. My greatest support came from my church and my family. I'm sure that some people who lost sons in Vietnam didn't have all the support that we had. We were fortunate in that aspect, yet it was still difficult.

I was aware of the AGSM organization, but I could not bring myself to join at the time of Bob's death. It brought too many difficult memories back to me. Later on, at one point, I was going to volunteer at the Veterans Hospital, but I just couldn't bring myself to do that—even then. No matter how much support you get from others, you're still the one facing the loss, not anyone else. But you get through it. You have to. It's a long road, and on certain days it can be rough. I look back at moments and ask myself— Has it been 40 years? It doesn't seem possible! He was only 21 when he left.

I've often wondered how we would have dealt with the situation if our son had returned home severely injured. A young man named Marty lived on Grand Island and served in Vietnam at the same time my son did. At one point, Bob had a problem with his back, and was having it checked out on a hospital ship, when he ran into Marty. Chances were quite small that two kids from the Island with a population of about 10,000 would happen to meet in the same hospital off the coast of Vietnam, but they did. Marty was in the hospital because his back was badly injured. As a result, he was paralyzed from the waist down. Despite his confinement to a wheel chair, he married, had a family, ran for a political office and served as town supervisor for two years. Due to health complications he passed away a few years ago when he was in his fifties. Yet he returned home and lived an additional 30 years, unlike our son. But it is best not to hang onto these thoughts for the rest of my life either. We knew his parents well and I'm sure it must've been very difficult for them. I think of how they must have felt as they watched him struggle with complications and how he had to adjust in life. I can't say how well I would have done in their situation.

I look back at Bob's experience during the Vietnam War, and realize that there was a great deal of support for the servicemen during World War II that was missing during the war in Southeast Asia. For example, when I was young, I was editor of a newsletter that was sent to all the servicemen.

It had started at church one Sunday night when one of the men said to me, "Shirley, why don't you do something like write to the boys overseas?"

I enlisted the help of a few friends and we created a newsletter called "The Islander." We acquired a typewriter, a desk, and two big maps—one of the United States and the other of the world. We put the maps on the wall in order to know where everyone was stationed. People from the community contributed money. With a combined list of servicemen from two churches on the island, my friends and I sent 155 newsletters every month during World War II. It gave us great satisfaction. The guys replied, thanking us, and informing us of what they were doing. They got in touch with each other—all because of our newsletter to them. They were always informed about the latest news on the Island, such as who got married and what was happening in the town. The newsletter was fun and went on for the duration of the war. It was a lot of work but it boosted the morale and kept the guys informed about each other. At times it was awful when the newsletters were returned indicating that they had been killed in action. My girlfriends and I ushered at the church where the memorial services were held. As I look back, I remember sitting through a service one time and saying to myself—I hope this never happens to my family. But of course, eventually it did.

I feel empathy for the American people who are losing their sons and daughters in Iraq and Afghanistan today. I also feel bad for the Iraqi people—for the losses they've experienced as well as the destruction they've witnessed. Aside from the right or the wrong of it, it's just like Vietnam, except I think it was worse in Vietnam in some ways. It's disturbing to think that countries can't get along. They always say that old men make wars and young men fight them. It's true. The cream of the crop goes off and never comes back.

If I dwell on it I could feel bitter, yet I still think of what happened to my son and wonder why things happen the way they do. Bob was such a good kid—never a problem in school. Granted, he probably could have gotten into trouble that we never knew about. That can happen, too. There are moments when parents simply aren't aware what their kids are up to. But if Bob had those moments, we never heard about them and we certainly did not read about it in the paper! Back then, I remember hearing about kids whose behavior was not so good, and I still hear stories about kids today. On the surface, it seems that nothing bad ever happens to them—and I certainly would not wish that it would. However, I must say I look back and ask how could such a tragedy befall a good kid like my son? I can only conclude that there's no rhyme nor reason for what happens in situations like these when parents lose a son or daughter.

Bob's absence has made it difficult for all of us, but I have my daughters' support. I consider myself lucky that Nancy returned to this area—all three daughters and their families live nearby. I think that they made a conscious effort to stay close. I've been blessed with six grandchildren and eight great grandchildren. We get together for football parties. We do a lot together. But *he* is always missing. It still hurts at times and I guess I'm not as good at masking my sentiments about it as I thought, because I made a comment about it one day. "Well, Mother, you *do* have three other children," my daughter said.

Oh! I better watch myself a little, I thought. It's a delicate balance when getting together. You can't be too obvious about how you feel at times, and yet at other times, you cry and try to hide it. Again, it is something you will never know until it happens to you.

****

As we finished our conversation, I asked Shirley what she would tell her son if she had the opportunity. She replied softly:

"I am so proud of you. Whenever I am in the store or supermarket and I hear a voice call out, 'Hey, Mom!' I still turn and look to see if it is you."

Shirley Luther with an etching from The Wall of her son, Robert

Corporal
John Michael Hens,
U.S.M.C.

East Amherst, New York

12th Marine Air Group, 1st Marine Air Wing

Quang Ngai Province, Vietnam

KIA: October 3, 1966

Age: 22

"Who is to say that what they did in Vietnam was not noble? Maybe it kept all the Chinese and Russians busy enough to keep their minds off coming over here."

- Marguerite Hens

I called local VFW Post 7870 to inquire about any gold star mothers in the Western New York area. The commander who answered the phone informed me that the post was named after Corporal John Michael Hens, who was the first Marine from East Amherst/Clarence to be killed in Vietnam. When I called the parents of Corporal Hens, they invited me over to talk about their son. After a two-minute ride from my home, I found the house number and drove up the driveway. An American flag flew from a tall flagpole that stood at the end. I got out of the car and looked around. A two-story, white aluminum-sided house stood on my left. Its style was reminiscent of the 60s. On the right, a large, old barn dominated the property. Its shingled roof, worn away by time, allowed birds and rain to enter. A weathered, gray split-rail fence, sagging with age and abandonment, caught my attention as it fought to hold back waves of waist-high grass threatening to overflow onto the lawn.

My thoughts were interrupted when Michael Hens' father, Ed, opened the door. He was a tall, thin gentleman with dark gray hair and a soft, deep voice. His wife, Marguerite, stood behind him. They invited me in to a cheerful, updated country kitchen that faced the back meadow. I stole one more glance at the meadow before following them to the living room.

Marguerite was tall, graceful and wore a short, stylish haircut. She had a formal air and spoke in a deep, controlled, clear voice. I learned that she had worked fulltime in the cosmetics department at Jenss, an upscale department store, while the boys grew up on the farm. Ed worked as a carpenter for a local home builder. They both led a busy life and all of their children had family responsibilities.

Marguerite and Ed had four boys: Mike, Thomas, David and Peter. Their first-born was John Michael, but they called him Mike. Marguerite pointed to her favorite portrait of Mike in his Marine uniform. She described him as six-feet tall, the tallest of their four sons. Studying the portrait, I asked if he was a serious, quiet guy. Marguerite burst out in a chuckle and began speaking.

****

He definitely was not a quiet kid. If he could get a shriek out of someone or a shocked response, he would go for it. One memory is crystal clear and I will never forgive him for it. When he was seven or eight, he came in the house one day with a brown paper lunch bag saying, "I have something for you."

I opened the lunch bag, and there inside was a mass of baby garter snakes. I'm deathly afraid of snakes and I thought I was going to get sick right there at the sight of them. He was well aware of how I felt about snakes.

When Mike was nine, he and his brothers became involved in 4H. My father, William Bachman, bought us a couple of horses for family use and were they nuts! There was one horse in particular that Ed could only get to go a certain distance from the barn door. When he got to that point, the horse used to turn around and gallop back to the barn. The only reason Ed did not get decapitated was because he grabbed onto the frame of the doorway as the horse ran into the barn. My dad bought a few more and they turned out to be nuts, too. Within a year we had 10 crazy horses and four boys trying to ride them.

My dad then bought us a beautiful purebred Morgan horse. After that we got rid of the crazy ones and started working with purebreds. Over the years we raised 29 Morgan horses. More than 70 foals were born in that barn.

As much as the boys loved the horses, they were a lot of work. There were stalls to clean and in late summer 1,500 bales of hay to put up each year. This taught the boys to have a very strong work ethic.

They also developed a love and appreciation for the horses. This paid off when it came time for the Erie County Fair in August. There they won money by placing in the equestrian competitions. Mike and his brothers also turned out to be big shots. Girls thought they were really cute.

My best memory of him was competing for the 4H Western Challenge Trophy. All young equestrians at the Erie County Fair coveted this particular award. In order to win it, the entrant had to place first in an advanced class that was offered just once each year. If a rider won first place in that class three times in the course of his 4H career, he could take the trophy home or, as they say, retire it.

When Mike was 15, he had already won the trophy in the two previous years. He set a goal to win the trophy for the third time, but his friends decided they weren't going to let him win it without some sweat. Many of his 4-H friends were older than he was and had stopped competing a few years earlier. They decided to "come out of retirement" and enter this championship class and give him some competition.

In the most advanced equestrian class, kids are judged on how well they manage all the horses in the class. They have to dismount their horse and be able to mount and ride the other horses. Mike's favorite horse was a mare named Plain Jane. She was like a machine, she worked so hard. Mike was her favorite rider and Plain Jane had no intention of letting others ride her, including his friends. They tried but could not get her to move like Mike did. He knew her well and he knew how to "push her buttons" to get her cooperation.

I was afraid to watch the competition that day for fear I would jinx his luck. I chose to stay back at the barn and prepare horses for the next class. It must have been a wise decision to remain behind and let Mike find the determination to ignore his teasing friends because he returned to the barn with the trophy. "Hey Mom, look at this!" He had done it! He won the trophy three times in three consecutive years. I hugged him with delight. We were all so proud of him—a 15-year-old outclassing his older 4-H friends.

A few years later, just before leaving for Vietnam, Mike sold Plain Jane to a little boy about 11 years old who lived in the San Francisco Bay area of California. Mike later wrote him a letter telling him how to "push her buttons" and get the necessary response from Plain Jane. The boy thought it was wonderful that Mike wrote him from Vietnam. Later on when Mike was killed, the little boy's family heard about our loss. Eventually, Plain Jane had a foal. The boy wrote our family, asking our permission to name Plain Jane's foal in honor of our son. He named the foal Corporal Mike. I would like to think that somewhere out in California this gelding is perhaps still alive. I was very touched at his thoughtfulness to do that in Mike's honor.

High school was a challenge for Mike, but the toughest part for him was getting up each day. I remember one morning when I kept trying to get him up. After several attempts, I finally took the mattress and dumped him on the floor. He pulled the top of the mattress over himself and went back to sleep. This always drove me crazy because if he didn't catch the bus, I had to drive him to school. I think he and his brothers waited until the last minute just to aggravate me. I used to stand there in the morning yelling, "The bus! The bus!" My husband can vouch for me on that one and they can all quote my infamous line, chapter and verse. "By God, you kids will get up early tomorrow morning!"

East Amherst was farmland when we moved here and we loved it, but our sons attended De Sales High School in Lockport, a private Catholic high school, 15 miles away. The bus ride surely must have been a chaotic one for their driver, Mrs. Burkhardt, but she was a wise lady. I think she was a saint.

On the way home, she often stopped at a nearby mom and pop store on a country road in Clarence Center. She let 30 boys jump out to buy candy or ice cream suckers. To drive those boys for an hour twice a day would test anyone's patience, yet as a way of showing their appreciation, they bought her a little transistor radio. They made sure it had good batteries and a decent station with rock and roll. She worked that route for years. No one complained.

Mike graduated in 1962 and attended Saint Mary's College in San Antonio, Texas for a year. At times, it seemed that he majored in skipping school and cutting class. He was more than an occasional absentee. He must have had around 80 cuts for 8 a.m. classes. He loved horses and wanted to be a veterinarian. Yet I suspect the early morning classes at college made him think twice. Not many veterinarians work the third shift and can go to bed at 7 a.m. daily.

After completing his first year of college, he returned home for the summer and fall of 1963, but was not sure what he wanted to do. He signed up for the Marines and left for basic training January 5, 1964. I remember vividly the day he left. I was feeling so blue. However, I went into work like any other day. While talking to someone about him leaving, I realized that my husband Ed had also departed for basic training during World War II on that same date. How ironic that a father and a son both answered the call of duty for two different wars on the same month and day.

Mike left for Vietnam in the fall of 1965. He was stationed at Chu-Lai, a Marine air base in Quang Ngai Province. He wrote frequently and I kept his letters. I remember his letters said that some of the guns and weapons they found on the North Vietnamese soldiers were definitely from Russia, indicating that there were more countries involved in the war than just North and South Vietnam.

With one month left to complete his tour, Mike volunteered to escort medics into the nearby village of Binh Dung, where they intended to care for wounded Vietnamese civilians. While heading down a path that led to the village, he tripped a wire on a land mine and was killed instantly. It occurred on his younger brother's birthday, October 3, 1966.

When my husband Ed served in World War II, men in combat often had an informal mass where they gathered to pray before going out on a mission. It was also a tradition for them to write their last letter and give it to a friend to mail, just in case they didn't return. Mike apparently did this, and we received that last letter after he was killed.

The Marines provided an escort from Vietnam. One Marine escorted his body to San Francisco. Another picked up the duty from there to our home in East Amherst. I recall this man as a most polite and excellent representative of the United States Marines. On the other hand, he was cut from the same cloth as our boys, who were not shy and could be real hell raisers.

The Marine stayed for the funeral and he was available for any questions or concerns we may have had. During Mike's wake one evening, as the family was walking out of the funeral home, I spotted some gorgeous Chippendale chairs that appealed to my decorating taste. As I walked past them, I flippantly announced, "I want that chair!" I never gave my comment a second thought. I had made it partly to break up the tension. We had three other sons and Mike's fiancée to bolster us through this awful time, so the remark was partly an attempt to keep the somber mood from oppressing all of us at the moment. I remained behind because I was occupied with putting together a list of the funeral procession for the undertaker. I later went out to the car and there was the beautiful Chippendale chair in the backseat. Unknown to me, the Marine and one of my sons had walked out with it.

In the course of our conversation, I later told the undertaker that I felt just terrible about the kids hauling the chair out to the car. I explained to him that I had instructed the kids to bring it back in—that I would never let them steal anything. The funniest part was that the undertaker was not the least bit flustered about the situation. He just smiled politely and said, "Oh, we saw it go out. We thought we would just add it on to the bill."

When the funeral was over, it was time for the Marine to leave for his next assignment. We never heard from him again. He was such a wonderful young man. He joined in with our humor and we treasured his support. It helped having an outsider. He never knew Mike personally, but the Marines are a select group who fit into any situation, and he was able to do just that. My husband and I will always remember him.

Our son is buried nearby in our church cemetery, Saint Mary's of Swormville. The small parish lacked a maintenance crew when Mike was growing up. As part of their commitment to the parish, Mike and his friends took care of mowing the cemetery lawn and trimming the grass around the gravestones. It was for that reason that we chose to have him buried there. I feel that he is close to home, and it is a place that he was connected to.

When we lost our son, members of the VFW approached my husband and said that, due to the fact that Mike was the first serviceman killed from the East Amherst/Clarence area, his name was going to be number one on the charter of a new post being established in nearby Clarence Center. The little mom and pop store that Mrs. Burkhart and the kids had stopped at on their way home from school became VFW Post 7870, the J. Michael Hens Memorial Post on Goodrich Road in Clarence Center, New York. Every Memorial Day the members of the post hold their services at Mike's grave and we attend. The post also made a financial contribution in his memory to Saint Mary's Church toward the purchase of an electronic carillon located in the steeple.

****

When I asked Marguerite what she'd like others to know about her son, she succinctly replied:

We were so proud of him. My husband always said that when Mike enlisted, he was doing what he wanted to do, like all the other enlisted men. We noticed how patriotic our son had become when he returned from basic training in the Marine Corps.

Who is to say that what they did in Vietnam was not noble? Maybe it kept all the Chinese and Russians busy enough to keep their minds off coming over here. Who knows what could have happened if that kind of police action hadn't taken place?

****

The evening ended. I thanked Mike's parents and stepped out onto the back porch that faced east. Darkness was creeping over the eastern sky, providing a serene backdrop for sagging fences, the weathered barn and overgrown meadow.

My thoughts returned to Marguerite and other gold star mothers whose spirits had weathered the worst storms in life. Parents like Marguerite and Ed had been committed to each other for over half a century. They symbolized a solid American couple who supported each other, embraced a work ethic, and upheld a duty to our country while maintaining a deep faith in God when sacrifices for our country required it.

Marguerite Hens

Specialist 4
Robert Mackey,
Medic, U.S. Army

Cocoa Beach, Florida

HHC 3rd Battalion, 1st Infantry Regiment,
11th Infantry Brigade

Quang Ngai Province, Vietnam

KIA: September 7, 1968

Age: 20

"People don't always know how to support those who've lost a loved one through a war. There can't be community support if people aren't aware."

- Genevieve Hamm

After landing at Orlando Airport, I drove to Apopka, Florida. I entered a quiet neighborhood with colorful gardens and located a small, one-story home. A pleasant lady greeted me at the door with a sweet smile. She was American Gold Star Mother Genevieve Hamm, mother of Robert Mackey, who had been a medic in the U.S. Army.

As I entered her impeccable house on that hot August day, I was welcomed by a cool blast of air conditioning. She showed me to her dining room table where she had placed a large 8x10 photo of her son, Robert Mackey. Other items included a framed box of medals, a Bible, and an American flag. I reached out, picked up the tightly-folded flag, and gazed at it for a moment. Despite my interviews with other gold star mothers in their homes, this was the first folded flag I had ever held of a fallen hero from Vietnam. She noted my awe, and began her story as I set the flag back on the table. I was struck by Genevieve's tenderness.

****

When they presented me with the folded flag at Bobby's funeral, all I could think of was how much it resembled a newborn baby wrapped in a blanket. The honor guard presents the flag just like a nurse presents a baby. It's about the same dimension and weight. The flag is all I've got now—my memories, this flag, and his medals—they are all symbols of my son's sacrifice.

He died on a Saturday and his body was flown home within five days. The day before his funeral, while he was still laid out, his last letter arrived. He described how he had just returned from the field, saying:

> We're so tired and so hungry. We just got back in from a skirmish. The cook said he's going to fix us something to eat, and now we can rest. While I'm waiting for him to get the food ready, I'm going to write to my mama.

He signed it and got it into the mail. That was his last letter to me. That night I stood there in the funeral parlor, devastated. I didn't want to leave his coffin. I just stood there. I felt all right as long as I could stand nearby and see him. Overcome with shock and grief, and in denial, I began to question certain things. I even thought that there could be many look-alikes in this world—that perhaps this wasn't my son. When he was nine, he received a scar on his forehead from a boomerang. There was no question. The scar showed that he was my son.

Midnight approached. I still couldn't go home. I wasn't going to allow him to be buried the next day without knowing what had happened to him. The death certificate came through unsigned. Nothing stated the cause of his death. When your loved one is killed half way around the world, you don't see what happened. I needed to know where he was injured. This was my baby. I needed to know the cause of his death. I wanted to undress him and see. "You can't touch him. He's G.I. property," the undertaker said. I suppose they thought it was something a mother shouldn't do, anyway. But I insisted. They relented and said they'd call Washington, but they were told the same thing—he couldn't be touched. The undertaker finally pressed the matter with the officials. It was after midnight when they finally got permission.

My son-in-law and the undertaker thought it would be too much of a shock for me to see, so they checked and did find out how my son was injured. He had been machine gunned right across the abdomen and it had hit the aorta. I now knew what took his life. Yet, I needed to know the circumstances surrounding it.

It wasn't until a month after the funeral that I received a letter from my son's commanding officer relating some things about him, and what he thought of Bobby, about what a good soldier he was. About a month after that, a second letter arrived, telling a little more. Finally, in the third month a detailed letter arrived, explaining what exactly had happened.

Bobby's company was in the village of Thuan Hoa, seven miles west of Quang Ngai. They had just come in from a skirmish and they hadn't eaten in three days. They were tired, very dirty, and most of all, hungry. My son died hungry—on an empty stomach. That always hurt me. Some people have wondered how I can talk about my son so calmly, but it's because the hurt's a part of me—I can talk myself over it.

My son and others were sitting around, resting on the edge of a field that looked out on a rice paddy. Another group of men, separate from his group, had just returned, when one of their men was hit in a distant rice paddy. One of their medics ran over to the injured soldier and bent down to assist him. The Vietcong opened fire on the medic also. This medic was wearing the Red Cross emblem, but that had no influence on the enemy. My son bolted. The company commander had called out to him. "Mackey, halt!"

The commander kept calling, but my son went on. Bobby was wearing his medic emblem and intended to help both men when he was killed. I don't understand how anyone shoots a medic who is trying to save the lives of the wounded. He had no weapon on him at the time. He had set it aside when he first came in from the field.

My family is Seventh Day Adventist and at the funeral service, the pastor quoted John 15:13 from the Bible: "Greater love has no man, than a man who lays down his life."

We know that Christ gave His life, but my son also gave his life for us. God doesn't *ask* us to make the supreme sacrifice, but my son did volunteer. He disobeyed orders, of course, but even then, I'd never scold him for it— that's what the medics were there for.

We were given the opportunity to have our son buried in Arlington Cemetery. I chose Rockledge, near Cocoa, however I still visit his grave and put flowers on it. That's where I'll be buried.

When Bobby was born, my husband predicted that we could possibly lose our son to a war. He had served in General Patton's Third Army Infantry and saw a great deal of combat in the Battle of the Bulge, Luxemburg, France, and Germany. He never talked about it, but every night he used to have terrible dreams. When I would awaken him, he'd tell me he was fighting Germans. I'm sure he was suffering from PTSD. That's how men were when they came home from war. He was overseas at the time of our daughter's birth. She was two and a half years old before he saw her for the first time.

We had Bobby after the war when my husband returned. Back then, fathers sat in the waiting room. The delivery room door had a little window on it for the fathers to peek in and see their newborn child. The doctor held Bobby up. "See Mr. Mackey? You got a little boy."

After the delivery, they placed me on a cart and wheeled me in to the hall—a makeshift recovery area at the time of the baby boom explosion. I remember lying there, ecstatic to have a newborn son, when my husband came over to me. "Well, there's fodder for the next war," he said with little emotion.

His cruel comment hurt me terribly. I didn't understand why he said that. But it hurts me even more now, because in hindsight, my husband was right—Bobby surely was fodder. After my husband's experience of fighting Germans, he believed our son would be fighting someone else in another war, at a later time. And sure enough, by 1965, we were involved in Vietnam.

It was ironic that Bobby served as a medic since he had such poor health as a child. Bobby was asthmatic. We lived in Ashtabula, Ohio, where winters were severe. Little was known about asthma when he was small, so every time he had difficulty breathing, I rushed him to the doctor or hospital. I'm sure they thought I was negligent. It felt like they were scolding me. "How long has this baby had pneumonia?" they demanded.

We did everything we could at the time, and the asthma was one of the reasons we sold our home up north and moved to Cocoa, Florida in 1950. Bobby was three and I was tired of giving a little baby drugs just to knock him out and then see no improvement.

The Florida weather proved to be the solution. Whenever he had an allergy attack, I'd scoop him up, run across the street to the beach, spread out a blanket and lay him down in the fresh air. I was not a trained nurse and I knew little about medicine but the breeze and salt air seemed to solve the problem. He no longer needed the drugs. I never imagined his asthma would later influence my career.

Bobby's dad was a bricklayer and contractor. He built homes for the noncommissioned officers on Patrick Air Force Base in Cocoa Beach. This was all before the space program, so our family got in on the ground floor as we watched the creation of NASA. Bobby was four years old. We always attended different events. When we were allowed in, we gathered around on the beach within 50 or 150 feet to watch the first small test rockets that were launched around 1951. While living at Cocoa Beach, we watched different rockets launch. Bobby learned a great deal about space. Some of the first rockets that were launched in the U.S. were under the guidance of the Germans who came over after World War II, bringing their knowledge with them. The Germans taught the Americans everything about space, and it was happening right in our back yard. This was Bobby's first connection to the space program and it later cemented his decision to make it his career.

He was always afraid of fireworks, so as we watched the small rockets blast off, I had to hold his hand. He was scared to death of loud noises. At one time he broke out of my grasp and I chased after him as he ran through the crowd. That painful memory is another ironic symbol. The last sounds in his life were those from a machine gun.

Bobby's allergies made it impossible to have pets with fur or feathers. But, he loved animals and wanted a pet. He began to pester me about getting a snake. Snakes petrify me and I refused. He begged me to let him bring home a hog nose snake from school. I should have negotiated with him on that issue.

I was alone in the house one day, seated near a hall, when a movement at the end of the hallway caught my eye and I froze. It was the hog nose from school. He had snuck it in, thinking he could hide it. I couldn't wait for him to get home that afternoon. In the meantime, I re-thought the pet issue and realized how desperately my son wanted a pet. The snake stayed. His name was George and I made it clear that if George was going to live with us he had to stay in Bobby's room. Each day, I peeked into Bobby's room. I finally mustered the courage to approach George with confidence. Eventually, my son and I both agreed that poor George must be lonely so we found a second hog nose. We named her Gracie.

In some ways my son was ahead of his time. He was a math whiz and loved what is now considered computer science. When he was 12, I walked into his room and caught him awake in the middle of the night. He had a pen in his hand, and I thought he was doodling on paper. There were always little pieces of paper lying around. He used to draw squares and circles with connecting lines. I couldn't understand what he was so interested in. Curious to know, I stayed up that night. "Come on and tell me. Explain this stuff to me," I said.

They were circuit boards. He tried to explain them to me. I patiently sat there all night listening to him, but all I got from the entire explanation was a headache. I have no idea where he got these ideas. I later spoke with someone who told me that back then, kids picked up comic books or little paperback books for a quarter and read science fiction stories like Buck Rogers, about the future and space. Perhaps he learned there.

As a parent, I felt obligated to know everything possible about his fascination with the "new math," so I enrolled in a junior college at Cocoa Beach. It was a special evening class for parents, but I never really mastered it. At least I learned "new math" at the third grade level! He was such a bright kid. I couldn't grasp everything that he easily learned. He always held scholastic promise.

Bobby graduated in spring 1965 from Forest Lake Academy in Orlando. Finances at the time dictated that Bobby watch his younger brother and sister while I went out to work. This delayed his plan to start college. But later that summer, events turned in his favor.

He went down to Cocoa Beach and worked at the White Castle restaurant. Most customers were either astronauts or employees in the space program. He began talking with each one and impressed them. "You're in the wrong place here!" they told him. "You need to consider working with us."

An IBM official came in, interviewed him, and they grabbed him up. IBM had the government contracts with NASA for space projects at Cape Kennedy. Since he lacked a degree, Bobby started out as an office boy. He was then given a parts delivery car to drive between the IBM and Apollo buildings. He loved his job. It was entirely related to aerospace. Once established, he began taking evening courses at Brevard County College in Cocoa. Bobby continued to advance in the space projects. The working situation was excellent and he had potential for a great future.

The first time he got his draft letter, he took it to IBM and they wrote a letter deferring him. He received three deferments because IBM said he was too valuable and that they needed him on their Apollo Project. They didn't want to release him to the Army. When his fourth draft notice arrived, he said, "Mama, I have to complete this military obligation and get it out of the way so I can get on with my life."

I was stunned. I believe that a young man has a civic responsibility, and my son was a patriotic person who came from a family of men who had served, but I didn't think that he would go in at this particular time. When he left IBM, he was promised a spot and a promotion with a salary increase when he returned.

He was inducted in Jacksonville, Florida, on October 18, 1967 and completed basic training at Fort Benning, Georgia. From there he was sent to Fort Houston, Texas, for additional training as a medic. At the end of March 1968 he came home for a three-week furlough, after which he was supposed to receive additional training at Fort Lewis before leaving for Vietnam.

When his leave was up, I couldn't bear to see him off, so his father took him. He left on April 17, 1968, Easter Sunday morning. I knew I'd be working then, so I said my goodbye to him the night before.

Tension grew when he called from Fort Lewis. "Mama, I've arrived at Fort Lewis but we aren't going to remain here. They're sending us directly to Hawaii for training," he said. This alarmed me. I saw the pace picking up and there was nothing I could do about it. He then called from Hawaii. With an urgent tone, he said, "Mama, we just got here and they're moving us out to Vietnam already." That was the last time I heard his voice. He died September 7, 1968—four and a half months after he arrived in Vietnam.

I was notified of Bobby's death while I was at work. Two men in uniform came up to me, one on each side and gently took my arms to guide me. It still hadn't dawned on me why they were there. Suddenly, it hit me like a flash of lightening. I stared at them, murmuring, "My son." I recalled a strange feeling. I remember deep in my stomach my womb literally jumped. It was something I had never experienced, as if Bobby's very own life had been instantly drained from me.

In retrospect, I believe there were a couple of factors that contributed to his decision. In 1967 the casualty rate soared in Southeast Asia, leaving a huge demand for replacements. The government was shipping these kids out as fast as they could draft them. They had no real practical training or survival skills to help them get through the war. After being contacted by the Draft Board four times, Bobby knew he'd eventually have to serve, so he felt it was pointless to continue getting deferments. It was shameful that so many boys born in 1947 like my son were drafted and sent to this horrible situation in Southeast Asia. They were sent over and just lost their lives. I think 1947 was the wrong year to be born for single males not in school.

It was also a shame that my son never got to see the Apollo crew make its first trip to the moon in July 1969 because we were so familiar with the development of the space program from its inception on Cocoa Beach. I'm a little more comfortable now when I see news about NASA on television, but at the time, I couldn't even look at news about NASA's great accomplishment or Neil Armstrong landing on the moon. To this day, however, I turn away if the news shows scenes of war.

And finally, it's a shame Bobby never got to drive his car again. He owned a Corvette Stingray, like many of the workers at NASA had. He'd purchased a used one but he intended to buy a new one when he completed his military obligation. In the meantime, he needed someone to care for his old one and he assigned me the job of caring for his Corvette while he was gone.

He treated that thing so well! I remember when he bought the car, he had it repainted metallic blue, with shiny speckles and it required 27 coats of paint! He was so proud to have it and he kept telling me about the paint job. I couldn't understand why anyone would want that many paint layers on a car, not to mention metallic blue! We kept it in our garage after he left. My job was to take it out and drive it, in order to keep it running properly. He insisted I run it every few days. I still remember his urgent reminders, "Mama, you must run it at least once a week."

I was so embarrassed to drive that car, but I did! I put sunglasses on and covered my head with a babushka [scarf]. I used to take it out, run it around on the streets, then get it home. Once it was back in the garage with the garage door down, I used to think, "Phew! Well, that's over for another week!" Yet, in moments like those, I was able to see life through Bobby's eyes and how he enjoyed things I never explored.

I never heard any negative comments about my son from people opposed to the war, but I still feel that people weren't knowledgeable of the Vietnam War, either. To this day, they still don't understand it. I knew people who had teenage children and these kids didn't know anything about Vietnam. They didn't even know that it's a country, much less where it's located. It makes me wonder if the topic is in the school history books. I spent a day taking some neighborhood children on a field trip to visit the Traveling Wall and to explain its significance. At the event, I explained the purpose of the POW-MIA flag and what it symbolized. People don't always know how to support those who've lost a loved one through a war. There can't be community support if people aren't aware.

I have been an active member of the AGSM organization for several years. They have always been an excellent group. I served as state president for Florida and I've attended the national conventions. A lot of gold star mothers don't want to join our organization because they think we sit around and cry about our sons. But nothing could be further from the truth. I've met many good people and my closest friend is also a member of the AGSM organization. We raise funds for charitable events, accept donations for worthy causes and help defray operating expenses. We have an informational booth at public events. I have a room of crafts to make flags or pins to sell at our booth when we attend veterans conventions or public events. One mother in our group is 94 years old and she still makes little flags to put on car antennas. We've also volunteered at the VA Hospital in Orlando. It doesn't bring our sons back, but we're doing something good for those serving. I served as chaplain for the V.F.W. Post 8152 after retirement until recently.

We're an active group. We have worked with the local Vietnam Veterans chapter to bring the Traveling Wall to Melbourne, Florida. Our aim is to bring about greater awareness to the public of the Vietnam War, and to remember those lost in it. As rewarding as our involvement is in such projects, it is hard for some who attend events there. As we stand there, the grieving Vietnam veterans who returned from the war approach us, sobbing on our shoulders, filled with such survivor guilt and telling us that they shouldn't have returned—but rather, our sons should have. They refer to us as their mothers, saying they want to be our sons, and they tell us they love us. They do everything for us. Various chapters of Vietnam Veterans of America throughout the country have been very generous and funded the cost for our meals at conventions.

After Bobby's death, I used his Servicemen's Death Benefit to begin nursing school. I would work, save money and then return again to school until I obtained my registered nursing degree. I was determined to learn all I could about medicine, especially asthma. I spent the next 25 years of my career at the Florida Hospital in Orlando, dedicated to the memory of Bobby. I think of him every day. Whenever I reach for my Bible, I always glance at the cover where I inscribed my favorite quote from Philippians 1:3. The quote says, "I thank my God upon every remembrance of you."

****

Dusk was approaching. Stillness settled in the dining room as we sat at the table where Genevieve had carefully placed the precious belongings of her son, Robert Mackey. Her faith had given her strength to move past his death. Genevieve's strength inspired her to keep Bobby's memory alive in her nursing career until her retirement in 1989. It also inspired her to console many returning veterans from the Vietnam War who stood at The Wall and faced losses of their own.

The author and Genevieve Hamm

Lance Corporal Mark Vanderheid, USMC

Tonawanda, New York

B Company, First Battalion,
1st Marine Division

Quang Tri Province, Vietnam

KIA: June 28, 1968

Age: 19

"I did all that I could do for my children and that's where my peace is."

- Lillian Schulte

As my journey with gold star mothers from around the country was coming to an end, a turn in the road brought me back to Lillian, the lady in the Theater of Youth in Buffalo. I never expected to meet her again; however, one spring evening while attending a meeting of Chapter 77 Vietnam Veterans and Associate Members, Paul Piotrowski, curator of the Vietnam Veterans Museum, announced that American Gold Star Mother, Lillian Schulte had generously donated various items to the museum in honor of her son, Mark Vanderheid. There it was. The name had found me. When I inquired about Lillian, Paul replied, "She lives just around the corner, up a few blocks." He gave me her phone number and encouraged me to call her. Her story would finally be complete.

On a sunny afternoon, drinking coffee, Lillian and I sat in her cheerful living room that looked over the slow-moving Niagara River and nearby Grand Island, N.Y. She carefully placed several pages of hand-written notes in front of her as she began to tell me about her son, Mark Vanderheid.

****

Mark was the second of four children. My oldest is Bill, and three years after him came Mark; I had my boys first. Three years after Mark, we were joined by my daughter, Ann, and six years after Ann, came our youngest daughter, Nancy. We lost Ann to cancer at the age of seven and then Mark at 19. I always say that I still have my oldest, Bill, and my youngest, Nancy.

Mark was born in 1949, after WW II, just before the Korean War broke out. At age two he used to hear people talk about it and he caught bits of news about the Korean War on the radio. I remember one day when he was so young, he turned to me and said, "I don't ever want to go to war." He said that more than once.

I used to assure him, "Oh Honey, you don't have to go to war. Daddy went and fought a war for you." My husband, Bill, was in World War II and saw a great deal of combat in Italy.

Mark was a happy, enthusiastic kid who loved people. He'd shovel sidewalks for the neighbors or cut lawns. If someone was out on their porch, he'd ask them if they needed anything from the store since he was headed up there for me.

One vivid memory I have was when he was 15 years old. It was the day before Thanksgiving, when he suddenly came down with an awful pain. I rushed him to the hospital and it turned out to be appendicitis. He was unaware that the nurse was preparing him for surgery and he kept telling me, "I'm so glad that I'm here at this hospital because over at De Graff Hospital they would put me in the children or infant ward." He considered himself a mature adult, much too grown up to be placed in the children's wing. I never said anything, but I knew that the children's ward was precisely where he'd wind up when he came out of surgery. To make matters worse, when he came out of surgery he was transferred to a pink bed with sides on it like a crib. I thought to myself—My God, when he wakes up he's going to have a fit! If that wasn't humorous enough, I recall a nurse later telling me that as she was wheeling him up to the operating room, she had initiated a brief conversation with him in order to ease his mind. "Do you like school?" she asked him.

"Oh yes! I like school very much," he politely replied. She continued wheeling him down the hall, trying to distract his thoughts from the imminent surgery. When she asked, "How about girls, do you like girls?"

He replied indignantly, "Of course I do! What are you thinking—that there's something wrong with me?!" I still laugh, thinking how the poor kid got so defensive when the nurse asked him if he liked girls and he then wound up in a pink hospital bed.

He loved school and got along well with his teachers at Tonawanda Senior High. If you were to ask him what he liked most about school, he would say it was the girls. It was a cute remark but it was true. He was popular with the girls and he liked them all! They maintained friendships and later wrote to him while he was in Vietnam. I remember one day I heard him come in with someone, but I stood working at the sink so my back was turned. I thought it was one gal who came in regularly. "Hi Pat," I said as I turned around. The young lady standing there was not Pat. It was a bit awkward, but I made light of the mistake and politely greeted her. After she left I said, "Mark, where's Pat?"

"Oh, she's around. In fact I'm going out with her mother and dad tonight for their twenty-fifth anniversary," he replied.

"Oh, well, that's nice; and what about this one?" I asked.

"Oh Mom, I'm lying. I love them all. But when they get too serious, out with them…," he replied with a sheepish grin.

I used to roll my eyes and quietly say to myself, "Oh boy…." He was a popular kid, always surrounded by the nicest friends.

After he was killed in Vietnam, the mothers of these girls came by to pay their respects, and thank God they didn't all arrive at the same time because I remember one mother saying to my husband and me, "You know, I think if Mark had returned home, he would've married my daughter."

The next night a different mother would come by and make the same remark, "I think my daughter would have wound up with him eventually..."

I never said a thing. After hearing that statement repeatedly, I turned to his dad at one point and said, "My gosh! Who did Mark take after? I was always shy and you were always shy..." but that was our son!

Mark graduated from Tonawanda High School in June 1967 and began working at Acme Supermarket in town. I had no idea he was seriously thinking of joining the Marines. When he told me, I cried my heart out. His older brother Bill was in the Air Force at the time and that seemed to be working out well for him. With that in mind, I was cautious that Mark's choice would work out for him, also, but I really don't know why he ever made the choice to enlist in the Marines.

He wanted to pursue a career in law enforcement and had been applying to a police academy. Unfortunately, he wasn't accepted. They were accepting candidates whose fathers were policemen. I have never ever said it before, but truthfully, I think he was deeply disappointed and felt that perhaps his one dream in life was no longer within reach. I cried for nights knowing a Marine was most likely to be sent to Vietnam. "Mark, why?" I asked him.

"Well, I know I can't win a war by myself, but there are children over there that have never thrown a baseball or played football. All they know how to do is sail hand grenades. If I can do just a little bit, I would be happy," he said. He felt compassion for the Vietnamese children caught in war. The summer after graduation, he enlisted on July 31 and headed for basic training. He wrote home and said one of the first things he wanted if he was sent to Vietnam was to be assigned to a place where there were people of faith and where there were kids around. That was Mark. If there was something to be done for the less fortunate, he would do it. I think he enlisted with a deep commitment to people and by enlisting in the Marines he felt he could accomplish his goal.

My son was 18 when he left for Vietnam and his little sister, Nancy, was ten. When he arrived, he was stationed near Khe Sanh along the coast. The Marines were allowed to have picnics on the beach with the Vietnamese people. He wrote us saying:

> There is a little girl whose father is a fisherman and her mother is dead. She comes to the picnics and when I look at her, she makes me think of Nancy.

The following February 1968 he celebrated his nineteenth birthday in Vietnam so I sent him a cake. He said it arrived like it was just baked. It must have made him feel homesick.

A corpsman is the naval term for a medic. The Marines don't train their men to be medics; the Navy trains them and refers to them as Naval Corpsmen. They accompany the Marines and care for the wounded in the field. My son was not a trained corpsman, but he was like one. When the corpsmen couldn't get out into the field to treat the Marines, Mark went, if he was able, and he administered first-aid as much as he possibly could. He was recognized for this.

According to a letter of commendation I later received, Mark's company came under intense enemy fire on May 31, 1968. His company sustained several casualties. My son provided medical assistance to the wounded Marines near him. Discovering his platoon sergeant was injured, Mark administered first aid to the sergeant when three grenades exploded near their position. He was shielding the wounded Marine with his own body when a grenade went off, injuring Mark's arm. He remained with the wounded sergeant. My son used his weapon to silence the hostile fire. Once silenced, he then carried the injured Marine to a landing zone where he was later evacuated.

I look at this document, describing the shooting and hand grenades thrown at them, forcing Mark to set the injured man down, pick up his gun and shoot until it was silent. Whether it meant he killed somebody, I'll never know. What choice did they have?

While he was hospitalized, he sent a letter home with a picture showing where his arm was torn apart. When I read the letter and looked at this photo, I cried and cried. I thought of the other injured Marine that Mark had carried off to be evacuated and I thought—Yes, I sit here crying and the mother of another Marine is crying as well.

In that same letter, he said he was offered the opportunity to learn Vietnamese. They needed interpreters to interrogate the captured North Vietnamese soldiers. He declined the offer. It must have been hard for him and all these soldiers as they lay there recuperating with time on their hands in a hospital halfway around the world. They were so removed from their families, and their comrades were still out in the battlefield.

My last conversation with him was while he was hospitalized with the arm injury. He was allowed to call home at that point. I later discovered how homesick he was because different girls from town corresponded with him. After my son called, he wrote one girl and confided,

> I was doing pretty well over here until I called home. Suddenly I got so homesick. I told my Commanding Officer that I just wanted to go back to my company and be with my buddies.

He was released later on and returned to his company.

A month later we were notified. I remember the day plainly. It was 8 a.m., on a Monday morning when the notice came. We were just getting ready to begin the day. Bill, Mark's dad, had just pulled the ladder out of the garage to finish painting the house. He had only the front to finish. When Bill began the project, I wanted him to start the front first, but he said, "No, I'm starting the back, and then I'm coming around to both sides, then the front. That way I'll know that I have to finish it." I still wonder as I look back at my husband's comment if perhaps he had a premonition. I think he thought—If something happens, I've got to finish that front.

Our neighbors saw the Marines at our door and knew what was going on. When the news got out, it was on the radio and television. The phone rang constantly. From that day on our house was never entirely quiet. Neighbors came, friends, people from church, Mark's friends—even customers that knew Mark from the Acme Supermarket who we never met, came by and wanted to give their condolences. Many of those people wrote him and sent him care packages. "What a wonderful young man...." they all commented.

We had to wait 10 days for the return of his body. The outpouring of love and the caring was unbelievable. We had no support groups back then, but we certainly got our support. The phone and doorbell rang constantly. One of my friends came to the house four times that day. The last time she came, she brought homemade sticky buns that she had baked. When she came in, she handed me them, put her arms around me, held me tight and said, "I know this is the fourth time that I've been back, but I just can't stay home. I just want to be with you, if that's okay." She stayed until late that evening. People we never even knew came by. All my neighbors sent meals over. My family never would've eaten because I never thought of cooking. So many people sent us food that my girlfriends began organizing it when they saw what was happening. They made lists of the donors, marked the dishes with their names on them and then had to find refrigerators to place it in.

Mark's death was devastating to us. Yet his decision to serve our country and give his life is still felt through the loving people who have come into our lives over the past 40 years. Their kindness and concern for our welfare profoundly affected us. One such person was Major Jim Poland who had the unfortunate responsibility of notifying us about Mark's death. That was the first time we met him. Our oldest son was in the Air Force at the time and came home on emergency leave. Jim was good company for my husband and son. He never knew Mark, yet he frequently returned that summer to bring papers that needed signing or to present us with medals. I often invited him to stay for dinner. I told him he should come by any time and he was always welcome. I felt highly complemented when he said that he had been in many homes, but never one like this. "I can tell that the love is genuine, I can't believe the outpouring of love and concern for you and your family," he added.

He wrote to his family about us and then he asked us if he could bring his wife, Ruth, to meet me. We met and became good friends. When Jim had to return to Vietnam, she called and asked if she could visit when she was in the area. They are wonderful people and I still hear from them after all these years. He became a colonel and was a wonderful Christian man.

My family and I didn't have any counseling at the time because it didn't exist. My real support came from my church and my family. We're people of faith and have always been involved in our church. I taught Sunday school, so my kids always took a great interest in Bible stories which they found meaningful. Mark was active in the youth group as well as Sunday school. I endured the tragedy of his death by witnessing the love that God showed for my family and me at the time. That proved to be the greatest support. My children were very good through all this and I was very proud of them.

We were never alone for two whole years. Our house had company every single day and every night. Mark's friends frequently stopped by our house. One evening friends from his graduating class came to visit. They wanted to put a memorial in our church in his honor and said, "We don't want to put anything in the church that will ever be stepped on or worn out." They installed a beautiful stained glass window. This was 1968, the days of the hippies, but believe me, these kids weren't hippies. They believed in God and you would not believe the service they planned. The lead singer studied music and had an incredible voice. The girls from her group accompanied her. Those young men and women put on a memorial service that even impressed our minister. Many of Mark's friends and their parents came to the service. My family and I felt so proud. I think people today often seek counseling because they are not too well versed in religion or in their faith.

People looked out for us. We've always flown our flag and when we were painting the front of the house, my husband took the flag holder down. We had so many neighbors call to tell us that our flag wasn't up. Someone once asked how many flags we used in a year! It depended on the wind or the sun and how frayed they got. People donated flags to us in memory of our son.

Mark's friends, who presented the window at our church, came by one New Year's Eve bringing gifts for Nancy. They gave my husband and me a beautiful flag with the stars embroidered on it. I still have it; however I only fly it on special days like Christmas, Veterans Day, or Mark's birthday. Another friend of Mark's, Bill Litz and his future wife, also used to come by every New Year's Eve to visit for a while. One New Year's Eve, as they were leaving, I said to them, "You kids have fun."

At that moment Bill hugged me. "I could never talk about Mark before, but I'd like you to know that my friends and I still get together, but when we do, our parties have never been the same. Mark was always so much fun," he said.

I will also mention that Bill sent floral arrangements on Veterans Day with a card that says, "In memory of one that has gone, but never forgotten." After all these years, he still calls or comes by when he is in town.

At the time I lost my son, two ladies from the AGSM organization stopped by to pay their respects. They asked me if I cared to join their organization and I accepted. They were a wonderful group. I began volunteering at the Buffalo Veterans Hospital with other members. I spent most of my time on the hospital wards with the Vietnam veterans—all so young. We fed them, wrote letters for those who were incapable of it, or we simply talked with them. We did what we could for them. Sometimes we brought various kinds of sandwiches or had parties for them. Their favorite sandwiches were Limburger cheese and onions. I kiddingly told the other mother who went with me that the Limburger sandwiches could be her job—I would do another kind! Many members did their part. Back then, several World War II American Gold Star Mothers volunteered, but of course, they have since passed.

I recently read that some gold star mothers are actually taking trips to Vietnam, to see the areas where their sons were killed. For some of them this may bring a sense of peace; however, I don't think I could ever visit Vietnam. From my own perspective, I would say that my feeling of peace came in knowing that I did all that I could for my kids. I also feel at peace knowing the love and support we received from everyone at the time we went through our loss.

I don't recall any public criticism about my son serving in Vietnam; however, one unpleasant incident will always stand out. I was deeply hurt when someone told me, "Your son was stupid to go to Vietnam." I immediately got up and began to walk out without replying, but as I left I turned to her and replied, "He kept your son-in law from going to Vietnam because he had the guts to go." I thought to myself—let her think about that! It hurts when people say such things but what can you do? You can't poke them in the nose even if you'd like to!

Mark is buried nearby in Elmlawn Cemetery in Tonawanda. After his death, I realized how much he influenced others while serving with the Marines in Vietnam. I have a collection of three medals and a note of condolence from someone I never knew, yet who served with my son. I will never forget one particular day when I went to the cemetery shortly after my son's funeral. His grave wasn't even sodden yet, and there on it, was a little box. I couldn't imagine what it was doing there. I picked it up, opened it, and discovered three medals placed inside. Along with them was a note explaining that someone else had requested that these three medals be put on Mark's grave. I couldn't figure out who placed the box there or who the person was that wanted the medals to be placed there. I felt honored by this kind act toward my son yet puzzled because the note wasn't signed.

I left the cemetery wondering who knew Mark that was serving in the military at that time. After thinking about it, I remembered his close friend, Larry Kimball, who Mark graduated with. Larry entered the Navy and trained to be a corpsman. He was home on leave from Vietnam at the time, so I called him. "Yes, I put those medals there," he said before I could even ask him.

Larry explained that on his flight back, he struck up a conversation with another corpsman. As they continued their discussion, they shared how they felt about a friend they had just lost. Suddenly they realized that they were talking about that same person—my son Mark. Although Larry had never met the other corpsman until that moment, they were both deeply touched by Mark's sacrifice and what he stood for. When the young man heard that Larry was on his way home to Mark's hometown, he took the medals off his shirt, gave them to Larry and asked him if he would put them on Mark's grave. Larry explained that the other corpsman was from Mark's company and had worked closely with my son in Vietnam. He told Larry that although Mark had never trained as a medic, he was as much a Corpsman as he was a Marine. When Larry arrived home, he honored the other corpsman's request. Larry placed the three medals in a box and wrote a note saying,

> I'd like to express my regrets for your loss of Mark.
> I'm a hospital corpsman and it really hit me hard.
> This medal and caduceus were given to me by a
> Corpsman of the 1st Marine Division who knew
> Mark and asked me to put them on his grave.
> Again let me express my sympathy.
>
> Sincerely yours,
> A Corpsman

I felt so bad that Larry never got the other corpsman's name. I would've sent him a note expressing my gratitude.

Mark's friend, Jim Kelly, served with him in Vietnam and was with my son when he was killed. Jim wrote me, saying he would contact me at a later time to let me know what had happened to my son. I felt that it would be very unfair to the young man to have to relive it, especially since he was still in the war zone. I showed the letter to Major Poland and he asked me whether I had answered the letter. I told him that I wrote the young man and explained that I would prefer to wait a bit until he returned from Vietnam, so we'd be able to talk face to face. Major Poland said it was the kindest thing I could've done for Mark's friend because he was still at war and he'd have to relive it all over again. Unfortunately, I never heard from the young man again. I wish I could talk with him now.

Mark died instantly from head wounds. Due to the nature of his injury we were not able to view his body when it was brought home. I asked the undertaker if perhaps, being his mother, I could view him privately, but he said it wasn't allowed. I didn't realize at the time that they screwed the top down on his coffin, and the undertaker would have had to obtain a court order in order to open it. I realize it probably was the best decision, but when funerals or memorials are held and there's no chance to view a loved one, I think the loss is felt even more. Seeing them one last time is a part of the mourning process. Thankfully, Jim Kelly sent me the letter after Mark's death so I knew for sure there was no doubt that it was my son who had been killed, but I wish someone would've contacted me because I still have questions relating to Mark's death.

I have a box containing his belongings from his tour of Vietnam, but even after all these years, I never displayed them. Mark's dad suffered nervous breakdowns from the combat he experienced in World War II. Out of respect for him, I just couldn't display all Mark's items. It's not that I buried my grief or denied what happened to my son in Vietnam—I just couldn't live with it all—seeing the aftermath of my husband's war experiences in Italy and then my son's death in Vietnam. It's hard. At times I think perhaps now I might display Mark's belongings.

I have no regrets in my life as far as my children are concerned. When I say I was a strict mother, I was. Like my kids said, they couldn't do everything they wanted, but we as parents were right. The boys once said to me, "You know, we thought you were a strict sergeant, but you weren't so bad compared to the ones we had in the military! Besides that, we never had a difficult time adjusting in the service like a lot of kids did!" From my point of view, I feel that I did a good job. I did all that I could do for my children and that's where my peace is.

****

I stared out on the Niagara River. I didn't have to ask Lillian what she would like to say about her son. She quietly took out one last sheet of paper, cleared her throat and with a quivering voice, she continued:

If I could share something with the rest of the country about my son, I would say that he was a wonderful, happy-go-lucky kid. He loved people, and that's why he was doing all that he did in Vietnam. If I could tell him something, from the bottom of my heart I would say, "Oh how much I love you and miss you. And how proud I am of you. Love, Mom"

****

As Lillian set her notes aside, a golden afternoon sun came over the room. Our tearful eyes met. She had gone to great lengths to share her story. It was certainly worth my journey to hear it.

Lillian Schulte

Private First Class Bruce Carter, U.S.M.C.

Miami Springs, Florida

H Company, 2nd Battalion, 3rd Marines

Quang Tri Province, Vietnam

KIA: August 7, 1969

Age: 19

"My son's life did not begin until he died.
I did his dreams."

- Georgie Carter Krell

When I called Georgie Carter Krell to inquire about her experience as an American Gold Star Mother, she insisted I come for dinner, meet her family and visit the family's vacation spot where her son, Bruce Carter, had treasured memories while growing up. She felt this would best explain who he was.

In the quiet neighborhood of Virginia Gardens, just minutes from Miami Airport, I located the street and recognized the Krell home by a large green street sign on the front of the house that read: Bruce Carter Memorial Highway. Flower beds and rose bushes adorned the little house. I walked through the carport and knocked on the kitchen door.

Georgie, a petite, cheerful lady, warmly greeted me. As I entered, she introduced me to Bruce's step-father, Frank Krell, a retired Air Force Sergeant, and her youngest daughter, Cheryle. Unfortunately, Georgie's oldest daughter, Pamela, was not in town and could not join us. After dinner, Georgie and I sat around the kitchen table where she spoke of her son, a 19 year old Marine, who was posthumously awarded the Medal of Honor—America's highest military award for extraordinary bravery.

As she spoke, I couldn't help but glance at the kitchen door where I came in. Forty-three years earlier, two military officers appeared at that same door in 1969 to inform her she had lost her son in Vietnam. Two years later, in 1971, a second knock on the door proved to be as pivotal a point in Georgie's life as the first knock had been.

****

There's no doubt if he had lived, my son would have been a Marine Corps general. Before saving his comrades in Vietnam, he saved two other lives.

Bruce was my oldest. His sister, Pam, was a year younger and Cheryle was five years younger. Bruce was level-headed and responsible. One day while living in New Orleans, we were dressed up and preparing to go somewhere. Bruce was waiting outside with Cheryle when suddenly he hurried in with her. There she was in her best dress—with muck in her eyes, her mouth and down her front. Cheryle had tripped and fallen head first into an irrigation canal. Bruce had pulled her out. He was only eight when he saved his baby sister.

My husband worked on the Gulf oil rigs, so the kids and I were often alone. One evening I came in from work and said, "Bruce, I do not feel well so you need to watch the girls while I lay down." I went to bed with my clothes on and didn't wake up when I was supposed to. This continued for two or three days. He fed his sisters cereal and wouldn't let them out. I wet the bed which alarmed him. He called my friend, a pediatrician, and said, "I cannot wake Mama up." She told him to call an ambulance and have me taken to a hospital. I had pneumonia and was unconscious. I often shared these stories of him but it wasn't until years later that I realized he had saved our lives. He was always there at crucial times.

My husband and I divorced when Bruce was 12. My children and I moved to an apartment in Hialeah, Florida where shortly after, we experienced our first hurricane. Bruce was a Boy Scout and anticipated situations. I arrived home from work to find their bicycles and our garbage cans inside. The bathtub and every pot and pan was filled with water. I looked at the situation, sat down and cried. "You are really happy, huh, Mom?" he asked.

"What are you doing?!" I asked in exasperation.

In a matter-of-fact way he answered, "Well, we got a hurricane coming. The stuff is inside so it won't blow away and we have water for drinking. This is survival…"

"Goodness! I never thought of that," I answered. His common sense humbled me. For two days we ate peanut butter and jelly sandwiches, had no access to the refrigerator and couldn't take a bath or brush our teeth.

The hurricane passed, everything went back outside and the water was drained. I praised my son. I also remember muttering—Oh Mother of God, do not let this happen again!

I disliked paying rent. Bruce understood how important a house was to me. One day I announced, "I am going to save money to buy a house, so you kids will have to behave and take care of each other." I had no idea what else I could do. I worked three jobs at the time. Six months later I had accumulated $500 for a down payment. I managed with a priority list—the mortgage, electric, water and gas. Next, I decided who had the worst pair of shoes. One got the shoes and then I decided who needed what after that. Bruce understood it. He mowed lawns and babysat. If anyone complained or got off track, I emphatically reminded them, "Our house is here." I was as proud of myself as I was of my kids. I've built 50 years of memories in this house.

I also have vivid memories of my son's teen years. In our free time, the kids and I used to boat over to a family beach house in Biscayne Bay. It was Bruce's escape to paradise. He spent days fishing and diving for conch to make chowder. When he was old enough to drive, he became crazy over cars. He bought a motorcycle and loved it to the point that he parked it on the front porch every night. It drove me nuts. The huge tree presently on the front lawn was once a tiny sapling. I planted it to discourage him from driving the damn cycle up on the porch!

My son was not the type to get in trouble with the law; however, our sleepy neighborhood had what the kids called a Barney Fife for law enforcement. Every time Bruce came down the street, Barney handed him a ticket—out late at night with a noisy vehicle, no lights on, no license on him, returning after curfew hours...All the kids got tickets. Bruce said nothing about them. One day a subpoena arrived requiring my presence. I was frantic—a single, working mom with three kids and almost all were teenagers. I appeared in court neatly dressed with pants on. The court clerk came out and said, "You can't appear in front of the [female] judge in pants!" I thought to myself—I don't give a damn! I'll fix this. My girlfriend was with me, so we swapped clothes. I put on her skirt and she wore my pants. I went before the judge, listened to her lecture and answered her questions. I wasn't defending my son's actions, but she hit a raw nerve when she asked me, "Where were you all the time your son was accumulating these tickets?"

"Probably working trying to feed him," I replied. I pleaded him off the case but the motorcycle went up for sale. Bruce was heartbroken but the insurance was unaffordable.

My son took after me. He was fun-loving, sociable and outgoing. By his senior year, 1967-1968, he watched all but one of his neighborhood friends enlist in the service. He was lonely and restless. He wanted out—a place to go and something to do. There was nothing to keep him in this sleepy neighborhood. In the mid-60s Miami Springs was like Hicksville—a farm house with ducks and mango trees was across the street. I worked and my daughters attended school but Bruce needed more than this. He expressed an interest in the Marines. I never thought they would take him.

Sometime after I had divorced his father, Bruce visited him in New Orleans. While there, Bruce cut his leg in an accident with a saw. The wound required nearly 100 stitches. In spite of the injury the Marines recruited him in 1968. He had not even finished his senior year. I recall no community support when my son announced his decision to enlist. I do remember hearing, "You allowed him to go off to that war? Are you out of your mind?"

After basic training he was sent to California to learn Vietnamese. His only furlough was Christmas 1968. He landed in Vietnam on April 9, 1969. I'd like to share one of his letters with you:

Mom,

We're doing fine; moved in on top of a mountain for a week guarding this artillery post. After that, we go to Qua Viet for four or five days to rest. I've been here two weeks now and I haven't had a bath yet. I'll get one in Qua Viet. You may have heard about the airbase, Vandergrift blowing up. Well I was there when it happened. A helicopter crashed and all kinds of things went up. No one was hurt because we all jumped into our bunkers.
We get paid May 1st so I'll send you $50, OK?
If you're thinking of sending packages, don't unless it's booze or canned goods because it will get crushed or it will melt or spoil. We get our mail in the bush so we have to hump what we get and big packages are heavy. I'm serious about the booze—it sure helps. I don't get drunk because we pass everything around but it helps. Well, I'll be 19 in two weeks. How about that? Time seems to be going by pretty fast so I'll be home before I know it.
I hope to be getting some mail soon. I haven't had any in about a month. I got a groovy mustache and goatee started. Also my hair is decently long.
Write and let me know what's up. Tell everyone Hello for me and start preparing right now a pot of spaghetti

cooking by the time I get home.

I'm tired right now because I had perimeter watch last night and I only got about two hours sleep so I'll close now till next time. I love you and miss you. Be good and take care.

Love,
Bruce

We exchanged letters and tape cassettes. He came down with malaria in Vietnam and spent 15 days in the hospital. When they released him he tried to call home, but he couldn't get through so he made a cassette to let us know he was better. You can hear it on his website: brucecarter. homestead.com. Click on: "about Bruce."

Frank and I had planned to marry on August 15, 1969, four months after Bruce left for Vietnam. My son loved Frank like a father and was thrilled for us. He used to comment in his letters, "You're finally getting smart, huh Mom? You're going to marry the guy that loves you."

My girl friends had planned a wedding shower. I remember wearing white bell bottom pants with eyelet trim for the party. I was waiting for them to pick me up when there was a knock on the door. Thinking it was the girls, I opened it. Two Marines stood there and notified me that my son was killed two days earlier on August 7th. I slammed the door shut, locked it and wouldn't let them in. They left. Shock and disbelief took over. My son was gone; there were no details. As we waited for his body to be flown home, Frank and I were quietly married by a Justice of the Peace on August 13. I remember little of our wedding ceremony or my son's funeral 12 days after. I remember how I felt.

The past 43 years have taken me many miles from the day I lost my son. You must understand where my mind was when the Marines first knocked on my door. I was never given an explanation for Bruce's death. They never let me open his casket. I had no proof he was in that box. *Open the damn thing up! I want to see!* No. Not allowed. *Then why should I believe Bruce will be buried here?* Emotionally, I never believed my son came home. It was years before I visited his grave. As far as I was concerned, his body was still in Vietnam. Two years passed before I learned how my son died, so what could I expect when they shipped his casket home and there were strict orders for it to remain closed? My life was a blur for a long time after my son's death. Time is strange. It bounces off you at moments like this. I remember sitting here the day of his funeral. "What's the date today?" I asked Frank.

"It's August 25," he answered.

"It's my birthday," I replied. "Why are they burying my son on my birthday?" Bruce was buried at Vista Memorial Cemetery in Hialeah. I waited for details but there was still no news about how my son died. I only knew he was not here. I was 39 when I lost Bruce. For years I did not celebrate my birthday.

Parents aren't the only ones who grieve the loss of their child. Siblings suffer the loss as well. At the time of Bruce's death, Pam had moved out, but poor Cheryle was 14. Lord, I was hard on her. The indescribable agony rendered me nearly incapable of helping her deal with the loss of her brother. I was here but I wasn't here. There was no counseling or support groups for families. I kept thinking—poor me. Pity me. Why did you do this to me, God?

About two years after I lost Bruce, two events occurred that began to release me from this nightmare. First, a neighbor stepped in to my life. Then, two men from the military appeared at my door for a second time.

My neighbor, Doris O'Rourke, who also lost her son in Vietnam, invited me to an American Gold Star Mothers meeting in Miami. At first, I refused to go. I thought—if I have no proof that my son came home and all they sent me was an empty box, why should I join this organization? I gave in and began attending the meetings, yet I told myself—I will join the chapter, but no one is going to make me do anything with all these old ladies!

A couple of members who volunteered at the Miami VA Hospital invited me to join them. I declined their offer. I was not ready to go down there; I didn't want any part of this organization and felt dragged there. But once again, I gave in.

I began by assisting patients who were unable to feed themselves due to injuries or strokes. Most people are unaware that these kids suffered strokes in Vietnam or returned home and suffered them. In helping patients like this, I was instrumental in founding the Silver Spoons program. Volunteers wore green jackets with a silver spoon pin and carried a green tray through the food line with a list of the patient's food choices. I travelled to numerous VA hospitals throughout the country, promoting the program. Unfortunately, as I chaired other committees in the American Gold Star Mothers organization, I couldn't keep the program going and I don't have the energy to restart it again! But to this day, when I walk into the Miami VA Hospital, they still call me "Silver Spoons." Other activities proved to be just as rewarding that helped me come to terms with my grief

We organized day trips for patients who were able to get out for a few hours. My daughters were wonderfully supportive of my involvement in the American Gold Star Mothers organization. I never imagined I would dedicate 40 years of my life to Bruce's memory by advocating for veterans. National headquarters records our volunteer time; I have given more than 15,000 hours of service.

In retrospect, it was a long time before I accepted my son's death, and I was a bitter person for years after losing him. I'd never care to relive those first two years, yet something else occurred that began to lift my spirits from despair, giving me a cautious optimism that I could get through this. I had been doing volunteer activities for several months in honor of my son when the second unexpected event occurred.

One evening, two years after Bruce's death, Frank and I were sitting at the kitchen table when there was a knock on the door. The old door had been replaced with one that had a window. I was shocked and surprised to see two Marines standing there and I thought to myself—*What the hell do you want? Go away. I have no more kids for you.* Frank let them in and they spoke at length. I have an entire cabinet of medals my son earned, so I paid little attention to the conversation until I heard them say, *The Medal of Honor.* I looked at Frank and asked, "Is that as high as they go?" He nodded. I turned to the Marines and replied, "Well it's about time you understood how good Bruce was. Yes, I will take it."

I finally discovered what happened to my son—he threw himself on a grenade to save his comrades. He'd now be recognized for his sacrifice. I had always feared that Bruce's name would be just one of many among the casualty records of American history. I used to ask myself—*Who will remember my son's sacrifice? Who?* Yet by accepting the medal for him, I thought—*Aha! They will never forget you now, Bruce!* I knew his name would be in books. I read everything I could find on this prestigious medal. On September 9, 1971, I went to Washington and accepted the Medal of

Honor presented to my son posthumously.

Joining the AGSM organization and seeing my son honored for his sacrifice helped me deal with my grief. In the late 70s, I attended the AGSM national convention in Washington, D.C. Every year, our organization's president places a wreath at the Tomb of the Unknown Soldier in Arlington Cemetery. The first time I watched her, I was awestruck to think that she placed a wreath in honor of my son and all others who sacrificed their lives for our country. I vowed to myself—*I am going to lay the wreath at Arlington... Bruce, I am going to lay that wreath at Arlington!* In 2001 I served as National President of the American Gold Star Mothers organization and indeed, felt privileged to lay the wreath in Arlington.

I have learned a great deal about the price paid by Americans as well as the Vietnamese people. Vietnow, a national organization of Vietnam veterans, is supportive of all Gold Star Mothers and they've honored us at various events. They have generously funded our trips to see Vietnam. Vietnow obtains coordinates from the Defense Department and, with the help of the Vietnamese government they locate the areas where our sons died. The mothers must be in good health for the trip—they have to be able to climb, carry luggage and take care of themselves for 17 days. Mothers who lost sons in the same general location are grouped together. For some it can be a healing experience. I wanted to see where my son gave his life.

Vietnam is a beautiful country. Farms and new villages have sprung up over the past four decades, yet four of us trudged through backyards and jungles to see exactly where our sons died. There are a few homes in the location where Bruce died; other than that, the area hadn't changed dramatically. As we walked through jungles and looked at the terrain, I feel fortunate in that I was able to get a feel for the conditions he and others fought in. The Vietnamese are most gracious. They are highly educated considering it is a communist country. Our tour bus driver was a college graduate, yet he could not get a job, so here he was, driving us around for a living. He pulled aside to show us a Vietnamese burial ground. Having lost a son over there, I had not given much thought to the losses the Vietnamese suffered from the war. I was not prepared for his answer when I asked, "Well, how many Vietnamese were lost during our occupation here?"

"Millions," he replied.

"I apologize," I said, and quietly reflected. We lost roughly 58,178 Americans but we, in turn, killed millions? Yes, we killed millions of

Vietnamese over there and they seldom talk about the war. Only the old people know it. They lived through it and remember—but they refuse to talk about it. The young kids speak English and want to learn more about their history, so they approach Americans and ask us to speak to them. Their ancestors died during the war. They have lost a part of their history. The trip taught me what was lost on both sides of the Vietnam War.

I served a second term as National President of the AGSM organization in 2008. First Lady Michelle Obama and Dr. Jill Biden invited a group of American Gold Star Mothers to a conference at the White House. They wanted our input on what more could be done for the children of those presently serving our country. There are numerous privately-funded programs that support military families as well as families who have lost someone while serving our country. The programs have excellent intentions and I would never put a damper on them or speak poorly of them; but, someone needs to address the needs of our country's gold star mothers.

Forty years ago, nothing was done for mothers who lost sons in Vietnam. No one came to my house and asked if my daughters or I needed help, if my bills were being paid, if we were eating or if we suffered with PTSD and needed counseling. It would've helped immensely if the government had a program in place that could've reached out to the mothers to see if they needed anything. Regardless of which war the U.S. is involved in, gold star mothers will always face the same crucial issues. It's vital to extend help to them when they've lost a son or daughter because if you have a mother unable to function, you won't have kids able to function either. War and losses dramatically impact thousands of families in our country. My second concern is for the gold star wives, those who've lost their husbands while serving our country. We need to raise public awareness that there are no programs available for the wives either. I'd like to see a government organization established or a private foundation where charitable funds and donations could be directed to provide temporary services to the mothers and wives of those lost in war. These issues have always been overlooked and need to be addressed by the government. Up to now, nothing has been done.

I've attended many events throughout the country, honoring our veterans. I remember hearing about a hospital named after a Medal of Honor recipient. I thought of my son and wondered why the Miami Veterans Hospital wasn't named after anyone. I took that question to

Frank Kovacs, my aide-de-camp and close friend who dedicated his entire life to the Marine Corps League. Frank had no answer. We explored the requirements of renaming the hospital after Bruce. Frank did 90 percent of the back-breaking work. We had to contact every military post in the state—the V.F.W., the American Legion and Disabled American Veterans requesting a letter confirming that they agreed to rename the hospital. We completed the task within four months in 2001.

We organized the paperwork containing everyone's approval and mailed it to Congress. Off it went in the mail. September 11, 2001 hit. Everything got lost. We had to reissue all that paperwork. Thank God we had computers to help us duplicate the material. The entire project was possible because of support from the Marine Corps League and many other people who assisted me. We waited for approval from the state of Florida.

Our Congresswoman, Ileana Ros-Lehtinen, was a phenomenal help. I got a phone call one day, telling me to turn on the television because the United States House of Representatives was In Session and Congresswoman Ros-Lehtinen had the floor. I watched her read everything she had received about Bruce and why the Miami Veterans Hospital should bear his name. The vote passed right there. We jumped and yelled for joy. We had achieved our goal. It took time, but we finally got the hospital dedicated in 2009. I'm waiting now for that big sign to go up on the hospital, The Bruce Carter Veterans Memorial Center. Little by little the paper work and business cards are being changed. Someone kiddingly said to me recently, "Hey, Georgie, there is a building downtown that doesn't have a name on it. Do you want to name it?"

"No, I've already done that. That's enough, no more buildings." I replied.

The Miami VA Hospital was the starting point in my journey as an AGSM volunteer. I feel deeply for those who've served and I want them to receive the necessary care, so it's important for every veteran to register in the VA health system. The Department of Defense has the military ID of every one who has served. The VA also has the military ID, but the VA has no way of checking the records of the Defense Department to verify that the person applying is actually a veteran!

Money that's allotted to the hospital from the government is based on the number of veterans registered with the VA through their hometown hospital. The VA allocates money to each hospital yearly, based on the number of veterans registered. This poses a problem because many veterans, some who are homeless, do not register. Also, homeless people do come in, claiming to be veterans when they are in fact, not veterans. The VA hospitals can not refuse medical treatment to anyone claiming to be a veteran. I can't stress the importance of a cross-referencing system that can bring up needed information on a veteran's military service so that only veterans can be treated in the VA health system.

Our country needs to know how neglected the Vietnam veterans were. There was no organization helping them when they returned from Vietnam. That's why they organized Vietnow, but they help all veterans. Everything that the Iraq and Afghanistan veterans have is because the Vietnam veterans fought to get it for them. We hear "Welcome home soldier. Thank you for your service, soldier." The Vietnam veterans go out there in boots and greet those returning from Iraq and Afghanistan. Vietnow veterans understand the heartbreaks and sorrows of those now returning from war. The Vietnow is a strong organization that has supported veterans and gold star mothers of all wars. I could call any one of them now and say, "I need you" and they'd be here in a heartbeat. Vietnow needs to be recognized for all its service to this country.

I never lost faith in my country but I did lose faith in the politicians who lied and did bad things. We're blessed to have men and women proudly serving this country. My dad was in the military, my husband Frank and my daughter Pam served in the Air Force and Bruce served in the Marines. My family has given to this country. Some gave all; others gave some. I have nothing left of my son's service except his Medal of Honor. The Military Museum of South Florida is under construction and it'll have a section for gold star mothers, so I've been collecting memorabilia for it. I want to donate Bruce's medal for display.

Now Bruce, I told myself, I am tired and I am not going to do anymore. I don't care to travel on planes, be frisked or have my luggage lost! But in May I'll attend the 50th anniversary of the beginning of the Vietnam War and the 25th anniversary of the beginning of Rolling Thunder on Memorial Weekend. I have a special white Harley Davidson motorcycle jacket and for one last time I will ride with the Rolling Thunder group for the state of Florida. They were born out of a protest about the POW-MIA situation.

Truthfully, I am not sure what I want to do next, but I know I want to be with my husband, Frank. He got me through the loss of my son. I could've never faced it alone. He has always been there for me and saved my life. When you've been through what I have been through, there's no doubt, on some days you feel like throwing yourself under the bus. Frank's family treats me marvelously, like I'm a saint. They're average people who work hard and love this country. Every year, they send me love boxes with $1,000 in it. I use the money to purchase clothing for the veterans. Frank's sister, Mary, keeps the family informed of my activities. Frank's family would also be here for me in a minute. Not many people can humble me, but the Krell family can.

I have many people to thank for helping me keep Bruce's name alive for the past 45 years. They've also contributed to my experience as an American Gold Star Mother. I'm also grateful to two Marines who, after 37 years, stepped forward and provided me with an account of my son's last moments in Vietnam. From that, I've gained a perspective on what Bruce really stood for as my son and as a United States Marine.

Rob Coughlin, a Marine from Baltimore, Maryland, asked me if I ever met anyone who served with Bruce in Vietnam. When I said I had not, he painstakingly researched online to locate those who knew and served with Bruce. A few months later, in 2004, a letter arrived. Here is the letter that gave me answers about my son:

Dear Mrs. Carter:

My name is Robert Haskett. I knew your son, Bruce in Vietnam and was privileged to serve as his platoon commander. Command in warfare has very few privileges and opportunities to get to know men in your command. Vietnam was not designed to develop a comradeship with the men in a command as men were rotated in and out of units as individuals. That denied them the opportunity to develop group loyalty and group integrity. This is one of the great shames of the decisions made by the command leadership of those who led the country in that time and era…

There was an understood distance between your son and my duties as their platoon leader. I did not share the moments in the middle of the night, when he and his best friends would share the secrets, hopes and dreams that each held. I did not participate in those moments of extreme loneliness, their fears that are shared before battle...Bruce never complained to me about being hungry, too cold during the rains, too hot during the days... Bruce spoke his own mind, stood up for what he believed and backed it up with what ever means he needed...

I asked both men, his squad leader and my platoon sergeant, to name one person they wanted to be in a fox hole with if we were over run. They agreed it would be PFC Carter...

I remember the day your son died and I would like to tell you about that day from my perspective... Mrs. Carter, I need to explain that when shooting starts, when men get ambushed, men react and do things according to their training, instincts and experience... I do not know any more than I remember. Others may have a different memory in small matters but we all recall the consequences...

We knew a large number of enemy forces were in the area... I knew we would be attacked that night and I wanted all of us to be on another hill when they did...It was early afternoon. I sent out patrols to scout the area and inconspicuously plot out the path we would walk after dark to the new location... It was your son's job to set out on this particular patrol...

Your son's patrol was out for 30-45 minutes when we heard the first shots. I grabbed the radio immediately, at the same time, ordering the reserve squad to "saddle up." The first voice I heard on the radio was Bruce's squad leader, yelling for help... Within minutes we were on the location and I could be there to take charge...The squad leader was trying to get his men to focus their fire on a tree line, just a few yards in front of them. Between their position and that tree line, was short grass, an open meadow of sorts and a stump of a large tree. The meadow was not large; they could have crossed it in a few minutes. The squad had entered that meadow and the point man had reached that stump when they were ambushed... Men were wounded and Bruce fell to the ground and began to return fire. Several in the squad began to panic but Bruce shouted instructions to them, rallied them to return fire upon the enemy position. With Bruce's leadership, the men focused accurate fire, each Marine doing what they had been trained to do... More men were wounded and that now became the priority, to get them to a safe position...I don't expect anyone that has never been in a situation like this to fully understand the actions, emotions and behaviors of those men that have been in combat situations. Men are changed forever in those instances. Most men find a way to survive, waiting for someone to tell them what to do. Other men find leadership and lead...The following events were told to me by those that were present at the beginning...Pfc. Carter immediately saw a need to do something. He acted with the best of what any man has—his courage and his desire to do what was right. He rose from his position on the ground and ran firing into the face of the enemy fire until he reached his buddies. He gathered them behind the stump, organized their fire and made sure the wounded were sheltered. As the men started to move back to the squad position, dragging one of the wounded, a grenade was thrown in the midst of their position. There was no time to think, wish or plan. Bruce dove on that grenade. As Bruce died, his men lived...I arrived on scene and took over the leadership. We battled and fought until the enemy retreated. By late afternoon we arrived back to our defense perimeter. Bruce's body was placed in a rubberized body bag and placed close to where the helicopter would land. I was in the state of recovering from the worst emotions of dealing with combat losses. I knew that I had lost one of my best men.

As I called the men up to my area and began to get the story of what had happened, I noticed that members of the squad and the entire platoon began to walk by his body, pause and move on. From the moment of returning from the ambush site until his body was flown out the next day, he was never alone. I had never seen that before or after, that respect for a fellow Marine…One or more of his friends and fellow Marines stood or sat with him… The platoon went about their duties silently and quietly…I watched as men would walk past his body bag and stop for a moment, doing or saying what they needed to do. I watched as two men stopped, kneeled and said a prayer. I watched some men stop, unzip the bag a tiny bit and place some object in with Bruce. We all knew an extraordinary man and Marine had died. I interviewed each man about what they had seen and done. They told me the story of Pfc. Carter's actions and deeds. In my own needs and in the shock and sadness that I felt, I fully realized why I knew that this man was special. There were fire fights throughout that area, affecting many units. No helicopters were available to come and pick up your son's body until the afternoon of the next day. The combat was so intense that only the critically wounded men could be taken out. I was now aware how hard his death had affected everyone. His squad was stunned. I knew the next day I would write your son's story. I would make it a priority to get it to those that could really honor him…The next morning…I tried to document your son's actions. It was not hard to write; what was difficult was leaving out who your son was—the man he was with his friends, the man who challenged his superiors to become better, the man who challenged his leaders to use common sense out of insane situations. I had to leave out so much of who your son was and stay within the guidelines for writing combat recommendations. THAT was difficult to do. I sent my recommendation for Pfc. Carter to my commanding officer. That was the last I knew about the letter... In the afternoon I managed to get a med-a-vac chopper to land and pick up our wounded with Bruce's body. That was the last I saw your son's body. I watched with great pride, then joined as the men stood and saluted while the chopper rose into the air, went down the valley and out of sight...Years later I was reading a list of Medal of Honor Recipients and saw his name. I felt a peace within myself, a long time waiting for it...I have never spoken to many people about my experiences in Vietnam. I knew that they would listen but never understand the impact nor the emotional toil combat brings to a man. I have made an exception concerning your son and his story. I have told Bruce's story to hundreds of kids as I was teaching, coaching them to be bigger than the self-imposed limits they placed upon themselves...I know that through your son, many men lived and were inspired to do better in their lives, as was I. Your loss was other men's gain. That, I apologize for, and I remain sorry that you lost Bruce so many years ago. I have always tried to understand, but no one can explain the sense of events like this...I can tell you that I have led my life trying to live up to the ideals your son demonstrated when he gave his life for others.

My wish for you is peace.

Robert Haskett

I then knew why no one contacted me from Bruce's unit. They are alive and Bruce isn't. It's survivor's guilt. They can't face a mother and try to justify being alive while her son isn't. AGSM headquarters is located near

The Wall in D.C. When I was president I often visited The Wall at night. I used to watch the guys as they approached it. Occasionally I'd put my arm around one of them and say, "Let me take you down to meet Bruce."

"Is he on The Wall?" they would ask.

"Oh, yes. Let me show you where he's at." I would walk him down and together we would cry. Bruce. Born May 7, died on August 7 and he is 107 on The Wall. Afterwards, I would turn to the veteran and say, "Show me where your friend is. Let's find him." It's hard to do, but I was good at it; I have no idea why. Many gold star mothers couldn't do it. I stood there and talked to these guys. It always broke the ice. We would sit down and cry together. They would tell me things and later say, "I feel better now."

I used to assure them, "You'll be better. You will feel better."

I know I am different. My son's life did not begin until he died. Bruce was a young boy who volunteered in the Marines and was dead at 19. I did his dreams. This is the way I feel and maybe it's wrong. Probably nobody else thinks like I do, but if your son had died at 19, what would you have? You'd have a few dreams of him at school, games he attended and Boy Scouts. But suddenly, 45 years pass. You're still back there and what've you got? You're still back at his high school, at his games and perhaps with a girlfriend he had. But what about all these years in between? What about all that Bruce could have been? *I am who he could have been!*

****

As the first night came to a close, I asked Georgie what she would like the world to know about her son. She immediately replied:

A general once asked me that question and I have said it many times. "What do you think I have been doing for the last 40 years? My motto is, 'They are our children. I won't forget them and I will not let you forget them.' I stand by my motto, bury me by it, upside down, cross eyed—but you will not forget. I did everything I promised my son I would do. I had no other choice. He dove off the cliff of comfort and safety for our country—I had to dive in after him in order to keep his name alive."

****

We spent the next day at the beach house in Biscayne Bay where Bruce had spent the brief, cherished days of his youth. That evening I asked Georgie what she would say to Bruce now. Her mouth tightened. For an instant, a trace of sadness surfaced in her eyes. She looked down at the table and lightly slapped it, as if commanding Bruce's attention. A big grin appeared. Her eyes brightened as she looked up toward the ceiling and she began:

Oh, I'd be pissed at him! I know what I'd tell him. "Do you know why I wear these damn white heels, Bruce? My feet are burning! Do you know where I have to go, Bruce? I have to dress up in my uniform, go out and talk to all these people and tell them about you! Do you know, Bruce, what I'd be doing if you hadn't done this to me? Have you any idea what I would be doing? I would be docked on our boat somewhere in the islands or the Bahamas with my fanny in the sand, drinking a cold beer! I'd be living like a beach bum. *And I probably would have never done anything past that.* But my life didn't go that way. I had to pick myself up, shake off and say: I am not going to forget you—no one is going to forget you, Bruce. Your name will always be there. I hope you're happy, Bruce. You better be having a good time up there because – *(she slaps the table and sighs)* I'm tired!"

****

A soft twinkle appeared in her eyes as she looked across at me. Still grinning, she lowered her voice and softly ended her comment:

****

Bruce doesn't say much. But I bet if I get up there some day, I'll get my ears burned off!

Placing the wreath at the Vietnam Memorial in Washington, D.C.

Personal Thoughts

The impact of the Vietnam War will always resonate with me. It resounded as the gold star mothers related their personal accounts forty years later. Faded photos gave glimpses of young Americans in a distant land torn by war. Letters yellowed with time were gently unfolded and placed before me—softly echoing with hopes for a safe return. The letters were sealed with love from their sons, but the stark reality is the indelible mark that the war left on the mothers.

Veterans say that war is hell but it's not just hell for those who die in it. The far-reaching impact goes beyond the battlefield. Combat veterans returning home often discover that the nightmares of war follow and will be re-lived daily for the rest of their life, though family members never see or understand them. Mothers faced their own hell when their sons never returned from war.

The gold star mothers who shared their stories for this book resolved to preserve the memory of the selfless sacrifices their sons had made. These women lived quietly, yet they had a powerful impact on their families and on their communities. They guided their families with values and principles. They were bulwarks of strength and support as they gathered their grieving families close to them and honored their sons. Faith was their compass as they steered away from a life of anger, cynicism or self-pity. They embraced their losses with dignity, serving as models for us in our own dark moments.

They carried a story that went untold for decades. I am humbled to have known these remarkable women who generously shared their most private feelings. May we never forget what they faced as a result of our country's involvement in Vietnam. These ordinary women of extraordinary character wove a shining thread in the fabric of our history.

I can't think of a better legacy to leave their families, their country or the world, than one of love, gratitude and faith.

Linda Jenkin Costanzo

A Mother's Tribute

The late Virginia Dabonka, a former member of the Irvington AGSM chapter in Weehawken, New Jersey, wrote these moving poems in tribute to her son, her hero.

How Many

How many blue stars will turn to gold?
How many young men will never grow old?
How many more battles must we still fight?
How many must die to prove us right?
How many mothers will shed bitter tears
for the rest of her life through long lonely years?
How many families have shuddered with dread
when the telegram said that their loved one was dead?
Dear God above, let peace be our goal
so no more blue stars will turn to gold.

My Buddy

I've stood shoulder to shoulder with generals
And shook the hands of some prominent men
But I'd pass that all up in a moment
To have you back in my life once again

The President wrote he was sorry
When he learned of your death in Viet Nam
But how can he feel the hurt and despair
As only a mother can

Now your name is embedded in granite
On that black wall for all to see
To remind us how you and your buddies died
To keep this great nation free

Though my future may sometimes look dreary
With God's help I'm sure I'll survive
As proud memories of you I keep near me
And in my heart your spirit's alive

About American Gold Star Mothers Inc.

Those wishing to learn more about the American Gold Star Mothers Inc., may contact them at:

AGSM National Headquarters
2128 Leroy Place, NW
Washington, DC 20008-1893

Website: www.goldstarmoms.com

A group of American Gold Star Mothers. Georgie Krell is fourth from the right in the first row.

Chapter 77 Vietnam Veterans of America holds a dove release ceremony on Gold Star Sunday.

About the Author

A lifelong resident of Western New York, Linda Jenkin Costanzo has studied in Madrid and Salamanca, Spain. She has retired from teaching Spanish in the Buffalo Public Schools and is now a part time Spanish professor at a local community college.

Throughout her teaching career, Linda felt it was important to raise awareness in her high school classes of the sacrifices made by those serving our country. During the war in Iraq her students donated new clothes to the Wounded Warrior program for veterans at Walter Reed Hospital. They have often sent cards to patients at the Buffalo VA Hospital on Veterans Day.

She feels passionately about the environment, loves animals, and enjoys being outdoors. She's creating a butterfly garden in a local park with the assistance of youths completing community service hours.

She likes to travel and enjoys sessions with her writing critique group. When she's writing at home, her cats compete for the warm spot on her computer. Her best times are spent with her family.

You may contact her at:
P.O. Box 92
Clarence Center, New York 14032

www.sonrisapress.com

Facebook.com/OurSonsOurHeroes